Finer Cooking
with
Mc Dougalls

Janet Johnston,
who heads McDougalls Cookery
Service, is well known to housewives all
over the country. She and her staff are expert in
all types of cookery and recipe development. McDougalls
cookery books have always been popular with housewives
and this latest book includes basic information on equipment and
ingredients, recipes for cakes, pies and biscuits and a section
on cooking for special occasions with hints on advance
preparation. All the recipes in this book have been
tested by the Cookery Service staff, who deal
with many requests from housewives for
advice on cookery and home
management.

Finer Cooking
with
Mc Dougalls

Hamlyn

London · New York · Sydney · Toronto

The front cover shows shrimp and cheese flan, page 29
The frontispiece shows Dundee cake, page 47; butterflies,
page 43; gingerbread, page 48; plain scones, page 56;
butter fingers, page 58; Grantham gingerbreads, page 59;
Easter biscuits, page 62

Acknowledgements
Dishes and accessories used in the photographs
kindly loaned by:

Robert Carrier Cookshop
Habitat
Harvey Nichols
David Mellor
Casa Pupo
Mushroom table and chairs in picture on page 80 by
Arkana Limited, Bath. China by **Wedgwood**
China in picture on page 59 by **Wedgwood**

Photographs by **IAIN REID**

Published by the Hamlyn Publishing Group Limited
42 The Centre, Feltham, Middlesex, England

ISBN 0 600 36098 9

Printed in Great Britain by
Sir Joseph Causton and Sons Ltd, Eastleigh and London.

Contents

Traditional recipes 22

Sauces 22
Soufflés 25
Soups 27
Pastry dishes: savoury 28
Pastry dishes: sweet 32
Puddings 37
Batters 41
Cakes and buns 42
Cake fillings and icings 50
Scones, teabreads and biscuits 56
Yeast cookery 64

Introduction 7

All you need to know about nutrients 8
Labour-saving equipment 8
Weights, measures and temperatures 10
Roasting chart 12
Basic ingredients 13
Shopping guide 14
The store cupboard 15
Equipment for the kitchen 15

Cooking for special occasions 68

Wedding receptions 68
Christening parties 82
Children's parties 88
Cooking children can do themselves 95
Dinner parties and buffets 100
menus for 2, 4 and 6 people;
buffets for 12
Drinks 113
wines, spirits, fruit cups, tea and
coffee, children's party drinks
Quick meals and snacks 117

Basic methods 16

Pastries 16
shortcrust, flan, cheese, suet, flaky,
rough puff, choux
Cake-making 19
rubbing-in, creaming, melting,
whisking, one-stage mixing;
lining a cake tin, baking times for
small and large cakes
Basic sauces 22
white, pouring and coating, brown

Index 125

Introduction

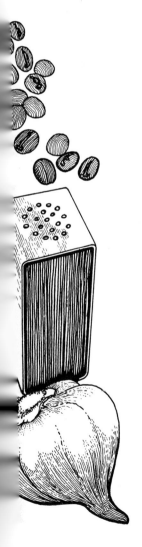

Our cookery book is dedicated to everyone who enjoys cooking—particularly to housewives, both experienced and inexperienced, who have plenty of enthusiasm and desire to experiment, but little time in which to do it. To start with, we have laid emphasis on all time-saving devices: not only on the most useful labour-saving equipment but also on efficient methods and making the best use of the many developments in modern food preparation. But that's only a start. No amount of space-age gadgets or time and motion studies will be of any use unless you have an up-to-date, really reliable cookery book to go with them. Here's how we planned it:

First, all you need to know about nutrients, labour-savers, weights and measures, temperatures and basic ingredients. Next, a section devoted entirely to the basic methods which occur time and time again in all cookery. We have grouped these together to save space (that is, saving all the space we would otherwise have taken writing them out in full every time they occurred in a recipe)—and to ensure they get the attention they deserve: each method is explained in detail and accompanied by a list of common mistakes made and the usual reasons for making them. For ease of reference we have marked the margins of these pages in colour.

Now for the recipes. We have divided these under two main headings: traditional, and special occasion cookery. Under the first heading are gathered together all the most useful and popular traditional recipes—British cooking at its very best. This is the section you will be using practically every day of the year! Special occasion cooking not only selects suitably mouthwatering recipes for weddings, christenings and parties of all varieties, but also helps with that most difficult and time-consuming of tasks—planning. Advance preparation, timing, calculating quantities: all the tiresome details of catering are worked out down to the last cup of coffee so that you, the hostess, can enjoy your own parties, and not greet your guests in a state of nervous exhaustion! So,

Happy cooking . . .

Janet Johnston.

McDougalls Cookery Advisor

All you need to know about nutrients

Whether you buy one of the attractively presented ready-made cakes, frozen, dried or canned convenience foods or serve home-made food, you need to be sure that your family have a balanced diet.
A few simple facts will put you right on this score.

There are 5 basic nutrients, their principal sources of supply are:

Proteins
animal sources such as meat, fish, eggs, milk and cheese; vegetable sources—wheat (including bread and all flour products), peas, beans, lentils, nuts

Fats
butter, margarine, suet, lard, cooking fats and oils, oily fish (kippers, herrings, sardines, tuna, salmon), salad oils, milk, meat

Carbohydrates
sugar, jam, honey, fruit, starchy foods containing flour, oats and other cereals, potatoes and root vegetables

Minerals (calcium and iron are particularly important)
milk, cheese, green vegetables, liver, kidney, bread and flour, dried fruit, cocoa, eggs, curry

Vitamins
A
liver, oily fish (see 'Fats' above), margarine, butter, cheese, eggs

B group
yeast, wheat germ, bread and other cereal products, meat—especially liver, kidney, heart and pork products—eggs

C
blackcurrants, citrus fruits (oranges, lemons, grapefruit), strawberries and other soft fruit, potatoes (especially new), cabbage, peas, beans

D
oily fish, margarine, butter, eggs

Vitamin C is easily destroyed by cooking—particularly over-cooking and keeping food hot. To retain this vitamin in cooked vegetables: do not cut them up too finely; never leave them soaking in water; never add soda; prepare vegetables quickly just before use; cook for the minimum time in boiling water; where practical, use the cooking liquid for soups or sauces.

Vitamin C is not stored for long in our bodies so an orange, half a large grapefruit or some other food rich in this vitamin should be eaten every day.

Daily meal plan
Milk   ½ pint for adults;   1 pint for children
Cheese   1 oz. for adults;   2 oz. for children
Eggs   1
Oranges   1 each day or ½ a large grapefruit
Meat or fish and vegetables twice a day
Bread   At least 4 slices a day for adults, 6 or
              more for children
Oily fish and liver once a week; bacon three times a week

Labour-saving equipment

The basic function of the kitchen is the preparation, cooking and storage of food with facilities for washing up afterwards. An efficient cooker, a sink (preferably with twin-sinks) with draining boards on either side, adequate storage space and working surfaces, a refrigerator or cool larder—all these are essentials, but there are many other labour-saving devices, some almost 'essential', others still frankly in the luxury class.

Dishwasher
These are best plumbed in to a water supply and a drain, although small models are available which are connected to the tap with a hose, and have an outlet pipe to the sink; they can be placed on the draining board or on a bracket on the wall. The plumbed-in type can be connected to the cold or hot water supply, provided that the hot water supply is adequate for the machine as well as other domestic uses.

Automatic dishwashers take 6—8 place settings, cutlery and glasses, and the average washing cycle lasts about 50 minutes. For small families the machine can be used once a day by stacking the dirty plates away out of sight after each meal.

If you are buying china and cutlery for use in a dishwasher, check that the pattern and handles will stand up to the temperature of the water and the detergent.

Home freezers
It is not essential for the freezer to be in the kitchen, but a dry place is best. If you store it in an outhouse or garage, stand it on blocks of wood. You have the choice of a combined refrigerator/freezer, a chest or an upright model.

The chest model has a top-opening lid and occupies more floor space than the upright model. Removable baskets and open trays are used in this type of freezer; storage bags in different colours are also useful for quick identification of foods, for example, green for vegetables, red for meat. Before you buy this type, check that you can reach the base easily, otherwise it may be difficult to use and clean. An upright freezer has the advantage of taking up no more floor space than a refrigerator. It has a front-opening door which makes food storage and removal easy, but accounts for marginally more heat-loss than the lid of a chest freezer.

A strong floor is needed, particularly for large upright models or a combined refrigerator/freezer.

Extractor fans

These are useful for getting rid of cooking smells and avoiding condensation. They are a great asset in kitchens which also serve as dining-rooms.

Electric food preparation machines

In this category are mixers, blenders/liquidisers and independent machines which do a specific job, such as grinding coffee and juice-extracting.

Food mixers

These can either be table models with a fixed 'head' which powers the beaters and whisks, or hand-held. The table models are the more expensive, strongly built, powerful mixers. They offer a wide range of attachments such as a blender, potato peeler, mincer and others to cope with a variety of kitchen tasks. To get the maximum value from this type, try and make enough room in the kitchen to keep the mixer on a working surface, ready to be plugged in. It is heavy to lift in and out of a cupboard, and the manufacturers provide a plastic cover to keep it clean when not in use.

Some hand models are sold complete with a stand, some offer the stand as an optional extra, others are only hand-held and stored on a bracket when not in use. The time that the motor can be run continually on these models is usually limited and it is as well to check with the manufacturer's instructions on this point. Hand models obviously have the advantage of being portable, so they can be taken to the cooker to whip up potatoes or correct a lumpy sauce. The number of attachments, however, is limited, so check on these before you buy.

Blenders/liquidisers

These may be bought as independent machines or as just one of the many attachments to a mixer. If much of your cooking involves making soups, pâtés, baby foods, batters and mayonnaise rather than cakes and puddings, a blender may be a better buy than a mixer.

One-purpose machines

Juice-extractors, coffee grinders, knife sharpeners, carvers and can-openers are amongst the many time-saving electrical gadgets which are not essential, but are well worth buying if your time is precious.

Waste-disposal units

These are electrically-driven pulverisers connected to the sink waste pipe. They will dispose of most things, but check with instruction card for any material which cannot be tackled by the machine. Waste-disposers are particularly useful for town and flat dwellers, whose weekly rubbish is controlled by the size of their dustbin.

Self-cleaning ovens

One of the most distasteful cleaning jobs in the kitchen is tackling a dirty oven. The latest development in electric cookers is a self-cleaning cycle: the oven door is locked and the oven is heated to a temperature of about 900°F., at which point the dirt burns off leaving only a minute quantity of ash. This most welcome innovation obviously adds to the initial cost, but the actual cleaning process is inexpensive in terms of fuel used.

The electric self-cleaning oven is the only cooker available at present which does the whole job itself, but other cookers, both gas and electric, are available with walls, roof and floor coated with a non-stick finish. Wiping over with a damp cloth removes most of the dirt, and any major mess on the floor of the oven can be soaked off, as the floor is detachable. 'Stay-clean' or 'self-cleaning' surfaces are also available. These are specially treated so that there is a continuous removal of fat splashes as they occur whenever the oven is heated.

Non-stick pots, pans and tins

The 'non-stick' description refers to a special treatment or coating applied to saucepans, casseroles and oven bakeware. Non-stick pans have been on the market for over 10 years, and during this time many of the initial difficulties, particularly their tendency to scratch, have been overcome. A light coating is usually satisfactory for cake tins, baking trays and other utensils used in the oven, but a stronger non-stick surface is essential for pans, particularly those used for frying. Until very recently only wooden or plastic implements could be used with non-stick equipment, but manufacturers now claim that metal implements will not damage the rough hard-base coatings used for many saucepans and casseroles now available. All non-stick pans are expensive, but the variations in price reflect the quality of the actual pan material itself rather than the quality of the non-stick coating.

Over-heating, rather than abrasion, now causes most deterioration of the surface, particularly if a frying-pan is placed empty over a strong heat. Non-stick oven-ware should be oiled lightly before use. Pans should be washed in hot water with a mild detergent, using a soft nylon brush if necessary. If water only is used an undetectable layer of food can build up over the base, causing the pan to burn when reheated. **Never** use scouring powder or steel wool on non-stick surfaces.

Autotimers

These have been available for the ovens of electric cookers for many years, and are now being fitted to an increasing number of gas cookers. It is worth taking the time to experiment with them, following the instruction chart, before putting them to the actual test—otherwise you may come back to find your meal uncooked because you have overlooked some vital factor such as forgetting to set the oven.

The autotimer mechanism is simple, but it varies slightly from one make of cooker to another, so always read the instructions carefully. Basically, however, you need to calculate:
a) when the meal must be ready, that is, the time the oven should switch itself off—say, 12.30 pm.
b) how long the food will take to cook—say 2½ hours.
c) when the oven must be switched on, that is, 2½ hours before 12.30 pm = 10 am.

You must also turn the oven to automatic and set it at the correct temperature.

Oven-to-table ware

This saves transferring food from ovenware to tableware, thus cutting down on washing-up. Some oven-to-table ware can also be used over a naked flame for preliminary frying before the dish is transferred to the oven for cooking and subsequently to the table for eating. This saves even more time, trouble and washing-up. Needless to say, it is expensive.

Plastics in the kitchen

Tremendous advances have been made during the past 25 years in the manufacture of plastic equipment for use in the kitchen. Amongst these are the manufacture of plastic bags and rolls of plastic film for food storage. Both are available in 2 qualities, one for use in the refrigerator, the other for the freezer. Firm plastic containers are also available in a wide range of shapes and sizes to make the maximum use of storage space in cupboards, refrigerator and freezer. These are also invaluable as containers for packed meals.

Foil

Rolls of aluminium foil are now an established kitchen aid for cooking and storage. There is also an excellent range of foil baking dishes in different shapes and sizes which are light, easily carried or stored, and washable.

Weights

The best results, particularly in baking, are obtained if ingredients are accurately weighed. Spring balance scales are inexpensive and reasonably accurate. Balance scales with separate weights are excellent but cost more and usually take more room. If you haven't got scales, the following will serve as an **approximate** guide, because tablespoons vary in size:

To give approximately 1 oz.:	Number of level tablespoons:
flour (pack down well before levelling-off)	2
granulated or caster sugar	2
rice	2
oatmeal	2
sultanas/currants	2
oil	2
cornflour/custard powder	3
cheese, grated	3
ground almonds (press down well before levelling-off)	3
coconut	3
icing sugar (unsieved)	3

Comparison between British and metric weights

British	Metric	Metric	British
1 oz.	28.35 grams	1 gram	0.035 oz.
4 oz.	113.49 grams	250 grams	8.82 oz.
8 oz.	226.89 grams	500 grams (½ kg.)	17.64 oz. (1.1 lb.)
1 lb.	453.69 grams	1 kilogram	2.2 lb.

Measures and temperatures

Measures are based on one of the following: the Imperial pint (20 fluid ounces) in Britain, also the gill ($\frac{1}{4}$ pint); the American pint (16 fluid ounces); the litre in metric countries, also the millilitre $\frac{1}{1000}$ of a litre (abbreviated to ml.).

British	Metric equivalent	Metric	British equivalent
$\frac{1}{4}$ pint (5 fl. oz.)	142 ml.	1 litre	1$\frac{3}{4}$ pints (approximately)
$\frac{1}{2}$ pint (10 fl. oz.)	284 ml.	$\frac{1}{2}$ litre	$\frac{7}{8}$ pint (approximately)
1 pint (20 fl. oz.)	568 ml.		

All tablespoon and teaspoon measures in this book refer to **level** spoons. Dishes cooked in the oven should be placed on the middle shelf unless indicated otherwise.

American measures

American recipes give ingredients in cups and fractions of cups: 1 American cup = half an American pint = 8 fluid ounces. The following are some approximate British equivalents to the American cup:

1 American cup of:	Number of ounces:
breadcrumbs, fresh	2 oz.
breadcrumbs, dried	4 oz.
cheese, grated	4 oz.
coconut	3 oz.
cornflour	4$\frac{1}{2}$ oz.
dried fruit	5–6 oz.
fats	8 oz.
flour	4 oz.

1 American cup of:	Number of ounces:
icing, confectioner's sugar	4$\frac{1}{2}$ oz.
nuts, chopped	4 oz.
oatmeal/semolina	6 oz.
rice	7 oz.
suet	4$\frac{1}{2}$ oz.
sugar: caster/granulated/brown	8 oz.

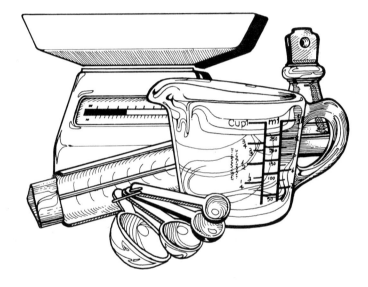

Comparative oven temperatures

Description	Gas mark	°F.	°C.
very slow	$\frac{1}{4}$	225	110
	$\frac{1}{2}$	250	130
slow	1	275	140
	2	300	150
moderate	3	325	170
	4	350	180
moderately hot	5	375	190
	6	400	200
hot	7	425	220
very hot	8	450	230
	9	475	240
		500	250
		525	270
		550	290

11

Roasting chart

Use this in conjunction with the instruction chart provided with your cooker. Where a choice of cooking times is given, use the longer time for thick and boned joints.

Method A
Roast for 10–15 minutes at 450°F., Gas mark 8, reduce heat to 350°F., Gas mark 4 for remainder of cooking time. This method is suitable for top quality small or medium-sized joints.

Method B
Roast at 350°F.–375°F., Gas mark 4–5 for the whole cooking time. This is suitable for large joints over 5 lb. in weight.

Method C
Roast at 325°F., Gas mark 3 for the whole cooking time. This is suitable for all joints—particularly the less tender ones.

Meat	Suitable joints	Methods A and B	Method C
Beef	whole fillet, rump sirloin, ribs, topside, round	15–20 mins. to the lb. + 15–20 mins. over	30 mins. to the lb. + 30 mins. over
	brisket (fresh)	not suitable	
	boned shoulder	not suitable	
Lamb	leg, shoulder, loin, best end of neck, breast	20–25 mins. to the lb. + 20–25 mins. over	35–40 mins. to the lb. + 35–40 mins. over
Pork	loin, leg, spare rib, shoulder, hand or spring	30 mins. to the lb. + 30 mins. over	40–45 mins. to the lb. + 40–45 mins. over
Veal	fillet, loin, leg, shoulder, best end of neck	25–30 mins. to the lb. + 25–30 mins. over.	35–40 mins. to the lb. + 35–40 mins. over
Chicken		20 mins. to the lb. + 20 mins. over	30 mins. to the lb. + 30 mins. over
Turkey	5–8 lb. in weight	20 mins. to the lb. + 20 mins. over	30 mins. to the lb. + 30 mins. over
	8–14 lb. in weight		20 mins. to the lb. + 20 mins. over
	over 14 lb. in weight		15 mins. to the lb. + 15 mins. over

Large turkeys are best cooked by method C to avoid over-browning.

Ham/bacon
Allow 20 minutes to the lb. + 20 minutes over. These joints may be boiled for half the calculated cooking time, drained, dried, and finished by method B, or cooked by method B throughout. Most ham and bacon joints need soaking in cold water for a few hours or overnight to extract the excess salt before cooking.

To test if a joint is cooked, place a skewer in the thickest part of the meat: the juice running out should be clear in colour. If it is pink, prolong the cooking time a little unless you prefer your meat 'rare'.

Basic ingredients

Flour

Self-raising flour is a general-purpose product, and many housewives use it exclusively with satisfactory results.

Plain flour is basically the same as self-raising flour, but it does not contain raising ingredients. It is used for mixtures which are not meant to rise, such as shortbread; those made light by the incorporation of air during the mixing, or by steam produced in the oven—batters, for example; and for rich mixtures such as teabreads and buns made with yeast.

Strong plain flour is especially suitable for bread-making at home; it is also excellent for Yorkshire puddings and rich pastries. 'Strong' refers to the quantity and quality of the protein it contains: it is milled from a blend of wheats which make a flour richer in protein than 'ordinary' plain flour.

Wholemeal flour is made from the whole of the cleaned wheat. It can be used on its own or mixed with white flour for bread and scones.

Wheatmeal flour has only a little of the coarsest bran (that is, the outer protective coat of the wheat grain) removed. Both wholemeal and wheatmeal flours may be plain or self-raising, coarsely or finely ground.

To store flour keep it in the original bag on a cool, dry, airy shelf. Plain flour keeps for 5—6 months; self-raising about 2 months; wholemeal and wheatmeal 6—8 weeks.

Sugar

Caster sugar is used particularly for cakes made by the 'creaming' method because its fine particles mix readily with the fat.

Granulated sugar is used for everyday sweetening purposes, for 'rubbed-in' cake mixtures, and many types of home-made sweets.

Brown sugars—demerara, barbados, soft light and soft dark brown—are used for all cakes and biscuits with a dark crumb, for example, gingerbread, parkin, ginger biscuits and often for Christmas and wedding cakes.

Icing sugar is used for most icings, for example, butter creams, glacé and royal icings.

Fats

Butter contributes its own special flavour to cakes and all other dishes made from it or cooked with it. Some blended butters are firm in consistency, which makes them ideal for pastry-making, though difficult to cream with sugar in cake-making, unless they are softened slightly first.

Margarine has added vitamins A and D, see page 8, by law. It is available in a variety of consistencies which lend themselves to different purposes: the firmest (and usually cheapest) are particularly good for pastry-making; the soft 'luxury' margarines are ideal for 'one-stage' mixing, see page 20, and are usually packed in tubs or double-wrapped; other types are useful for cakes made by the creaming method. Margarine prepared purely from vegetable oils is available if you wish to avoid or cut down on animal fats.

Suet is prepared from best-quality beef fat, ready shredded and lightly coated with flour to prevent the shreds sticking together in the packet. It is best stored in a cool, dry place in the kitchen.

Lard is pure (100%) pig fat. It makes the shortest pastry, but is a little difficult to handle on its own, so is often used with butter or margarine, both of which add colour and flavour to the finished pastry.

Cooking fats are mainly vegetable in origin; some are 'whipped-up' to give them a soft consistency.

Oils Liquid cooking oils are particularly useful for frying and braising. Olive oil, which is derived from juice extracted from the olive, imparts, like butter, its own particular flavour to a recipe. It is the best oil to use for salad dressings.

Shopping guide

Here is a general guide of how much meat, fish and vegetables you need to buy per adult person for a main meal:

Meat

For roasting with bone	8 oz.
For roasting boneless	5–6 oz.
Cold meat	3 oz.
Liver	4–6 oz.
Kidney	4 oz. ox kidney 1–2 sheep's kidneys 1 pig's kidney
Mince	4 oz.
Frying or grilling steak	about 6 oz.
Stewing meat with bone Stewing meat, boned	6–8 oz. 4–5 oz.
Chops	1
Cutlets	2
Escalopes of veal	1

Fish

Cutlets or steaks	1 of about 6 oz.
Sole, plaice, etc. for grilling or frying	1
Fillets	4–6 oz.
Prawns, shrimps	$\frac{1}{4}$ pint

Vegetables

Broad beans	8–12 oz.
French or runner beans	6–8 oz.
Brussels sprouts	6–8 oz.
Cabbage	6 oz.
Carrots	4 oz.
Leeks	8–12 oz.
Mushrooms	2–4 oz.
Onions	6–8 oz.
Peas	about 8 oz.
Potatoes	4–8 oz.
Spinach	8–12 oz.
Tomatoes	4–6 oz.

The store cupboard

A well-stocked store cupboard will make life easier. It should contain everyday ingredients and cans and packets which will provide a quick meal in an emergency, particularly in conjunction with foods such as eggs, cheese and bacon which may be in the larder or refrigerator. Here are some suggestions which can be varied according to personal taste:

Dry ingredients
Plain and self-raising flours, cornflour, custard, quick desserts, jellies, salt, pepper, mustard, rice, pasta, stock cubes, packet stuffing mixes, dried fruit, nuts, herbs, spices, sugar, breakfast cereals, biscuits, instant non-fat milk and instant mashed potato mix

Canned foods
Soups, meat, fish, vegetables, fruit, cream, milk, fruit and vegetable juices

Sauces etc.
Tomato, Worcestershire, chutney, pickles, essences, salad and cooking oils, vinegar, horseradish and tomato purée

Beverages
Tea, coffee, cocoa, chocolate, fruit squashes

Preserves
Jams, jellies, marmalade, honey, syrup, fish and meat spreads and pastes for sandwiches

Complete meals
Keep a selection of complete meals in cans, packets or deep-frozen, according to the storage facilities available. If you have a home freezer, be sure that some of the items can be cooked quickly straight from the freezer.

Equipment for the kitchen

As well as the large items—cooker, refrigerator, sink and cupboards, it is necessary to have a selection of the following. It is always advisable to purchase good quality kitchen equipment which will give much better service than the cheaper quality. Although it may seem an expensive outlay it will certainly prove to be worthwhile.

Saucepans and lids of varying sizes, according to the family
Milk saucepan, preferably a non-stick one
Frying pan

Chip pan and basket, if used
Steamer with ridged base which can fit over several pans
Kettle

Baking tins
Flat baking trays for scones and biscuits
Yorkshire pudding tin
Selection of cake tins e.g. 6 and 8 inches in diameter
Sandwich tin 8 inches in diameter or 2 x 7-inch ones
Flan rings
Bun tins, 9—12 in a set or individual tartlet tins

Cutlery
Knives—vegetable, palette, pointed chopping knives, round bladed for pastry, vegetable peeler, bread knife
Spoons—table, dessert and teaspoons, wooden spoons
Forks

Casseroles including oven-to-table ware, pie dishes, plates
Bowls and basins in assorted sizes, plastic containers for food storage
Graduated measuring jug to hold $\frac{1}{2}$ or 1 pint

Miscellaneous equipment
Cake cooling rack, can opener, cork screw, chopping board, cutters for scones, biscuits and tartlet cases, strainer, colander, whisk, draining spoon or fish slice, grater, lemon squeezer, rolling pin, scales, scissors, sink tidy, storage jars, pastry brush for egg or fat, refuse bin
Tea-towels, oven cloths, washing up mop and brush for saucepans, dish cloths

Basic methods

Pastries

Shortcrust pastry

8 oz. flour, self-raising or plain
pinch salt
4 oz. fat, for example 2 oz. margarine and 2 oz. lard
cold water to mix—about 2 tablespoonfuls

Mix flour and salt, add fats and cut up into small pieces using a knife. Rub fats into flour until mixture resembles breadcrumbs. Add enough water to bind mixture into a pliable paste. Knead lightly on a floured board, turn over so the smooth side is uppermost. Roll out and use as directed.

Flan pastry

quantity given will line an 8-inch flan ring:
3 oz. butter or margarine
6 oz. flour, self-raising or plain
pinch salt
1 teaspoonful caster sugar
1 egg yolk
cold water to mix

Rub fat into flour and salt. Stir in sugar and mix to a pliable paste with egg yolk and water. Knead lightly, roll out and use as directed.

To prepare a flan case Grease a piece of greaseproof paper, lay it on a baking tray and place a greased flan ring on it.

Roll out the pastry into a round about 1 inch larger than the flan ring. Fold in half, lift into the ring, open out and press well against the base and sides.

Trim off the edges cleanly with a sharp knife.

Press a large round of greased greaseproof paper, greased side down, on the pastry, fill with bread-crusts to prevent the pastry rising. Alternatively, cover with aluminium foil. Bake for about 15 minutes then remove the paper, etc. and return the pastry to the oven for a few minutes to dry the centre. The above procedure is termed baking 'blind'.

Cheese pastry

4 oz. flour, self-raising or plain
pinch salt
shake pepper
pinch cayenne pepper (optional)
2 oz. butter or margarine
2 oz. dry cheese, grated
1 egg yolk
cold water to mix

Sieve or mix flour and seasonings. Rub in fat, stir in cheese. Mix to a firm paste with egg yolk and water. Knead lightly, roll out and use as directed.

Putting things right

Did your pastry break up when rolled out?
The fat was over-rubbed into the flour—stop rubbing in a little earlier next time.
Did your pastry shrink away from the side of the dish during cooking?
Avoid stretching the pastry to make it fit the dish: roll it out a bit larger instead. Use trimmings for decoration or for making a jam turnover.
Was your pastry hard after cooking?
Use less water for mixing.

Suet pastry

4 oz. shredded suet
8 oz. self-raising flour
pinch salt
cold water to mix

Stir suet into flour and salt. Add cold water to make a pliable paste. Knead lightly, roll out as directed.

Putting things right

Did your dumplings break up in the soup?
Simmer the liquid used for cooking—do not let it boil quickly.
Was your baked suet crust hard?
For the crispest finish serve suet pastry straight from the oven or reheat it gently next day.
Was your steamed pudding heavy?
Make sure the water is really boiling when you put the pudding in to cook, and make sure the water used for topping up is also boiling.

Flaky pastry

8 oz. plain flour*
pinch salt
5 oz. butter or **5 oz.** margarine and lard mixed
squeeze lemon juice (optional)
just under $\frac{1}{4}$ pint cold water to mix

Sieve the flour and salt into a basin, divide the fat into 4 portions on a plate. Put one quarter into the flour and rub it in. Mix to a pliable dough with lemon juice and cold water and turn on to a floured board, knead well. Roll into an oblong about 14 inches long and 6 inches wide, keeping the sides quite straight and the top flat.

Mark the pastry into 3 equal portions without cutting it. Put the second portion of fat in small pieces over the top two thirds, then fold the bottom third up over the middle and the top one down over the other two. Seal the open ends with rolling pin and give the pastry one-half turn so that the folded end is to the right or left.

Roll out again into an oblong a little larger than the first. Mark into 3 again and repeat twice with the remaining portions of fat. Roll out once more and fold up as before, then leave in a cold place for as long as possible.

Use as required for meat dishes of all kinds, mince pies, sausage rolls, etc. For savoury dishes, brush beaten egg over pastry before putting into oven.

*Strong plain flour gives the best results.

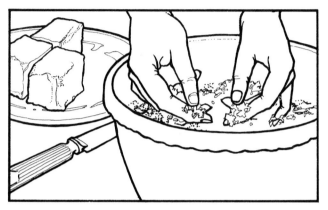

Rubbing one quarter of the fat into the sieved flour and salt.

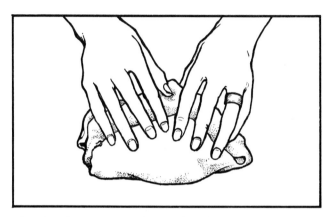

The dough placed on a floured board and being kneaded.

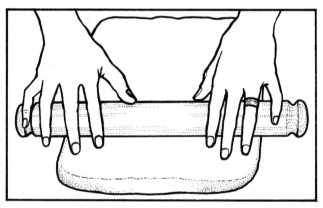

The dough being rolled to an oblong about 14 inches long and 6 inches wide.

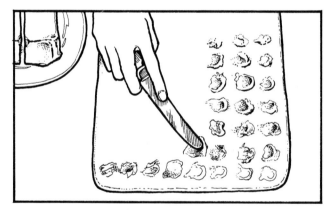

The second portion of fat being placed, in small pieces, over the top two thirds of the rolled out dough.

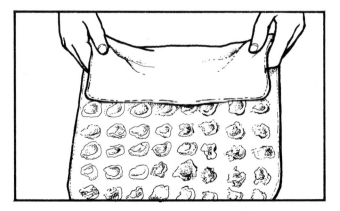

The bottom third of the dough being folded up over the middle.

The top third being folded down over the other two.

Rough puff pastry

8 oz. plain flour*
pinch salt
squeeze lemon juice or pinch cream of tartar
6–8 oz. firm butter or margarine
about ¼ pint cold water to mix

Sieve flour, salt and cream of tartar (if used). Cut fat into pieces the size of a small walnut and add to flour. Mix to a pliable paste with the water and lemon juice (if used).

Shape pastry into an oblong with floured fingers, then roll into a thin oblong on a floured board. Fold up lower third of pastry, bring top third down on to it, seal open edges with rolling pin. Turn with the fold to the left-hand side. Press 2 or 3 times with rolling pin to flatten. Roll out into a thin oblong and repeat as indicated above.

Leave in a cold place for about 20 minutes. Repeat the rolling, folding and resting as above 4 more times. Wrap in greaseproof paper, then a damp cloth and leave in a cold place for 1 hour or overnight. Roll out and use as required.

*Strong plain flour gives the best results.

Putting things right

Did the fat keep coming through the pastry, sticking to the board?
With rolling and handling, fat becomes soft—put the mixture in a refrigerator or a cool place to harden.
Did the fat ooze on to the baking tray during cooking?
Use a hotter oven to set the pastry quickly.
Did your pastry rise unevenly?
Make sure it is rolled out with even pressure and that the sides and top of the pastry are kept straight so that after folding it remains a true rectangle.

Choux pastry

4 oz. self-raising flour
pinch salt
½ **oz.** sugar (omit for savoury dishes and cream buns)
¼ pint water
2 oz. butter
2–3 eggs

Sieve flour, salt and sugar on to a piece of paper. Put water and fat into a small saucepan, bring to the boil, then add flour mixture all at once. Stir quickly with a wooden spoon until the mixture forms a smooth ball of dough. Remove from heat, add 1 egg, stir, then beat very thoroughly until it has been absorbed. Re-

peat with the second egg. Beat the third egg and add enough of it to bring the mixture to a velvety consistency, so that it keeps its shape when pulled into points with the spoon. Beat thoroughly before use.

Puttings things right

Did the mixture fail to rise in the oven?
Give it a more thorough beating.
Were your éclairs damp inside?
Next time prolong the baking period and slit one open to make sure the centre is dry before removing them from the oven.
Were your éclairs soggy?
Choux pastry can be kept unfilled in a tin, but as soon as éclairs, etc. are filled they start to soften, so fill them just before serving.

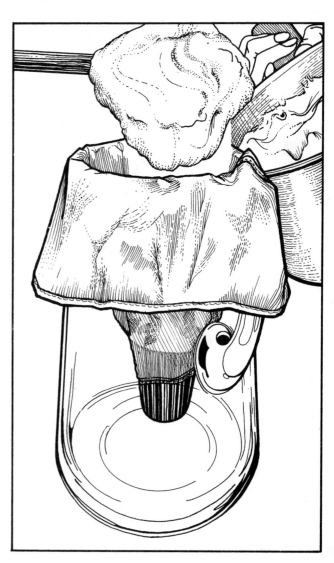

Filling a piping bag with choux paste; place the piping bag inside a tall jug. Turn back open end of bag over top of jug and spoon in choux paste.

Cake-making

Rubbing-in method

Sieve or mix flour, salt and spice or cocoa (if used) together in a mixing bowl. Add fat to dry ingredients and cut it into small pieces with a knife. Rub fat and flour between finger-tips until mixture resembles breadcrumbs, then stir in sugar, fruit, etc. Make a well in the centre of the dry mixture and add beaten egg, any milk and water or liquid that may be included in the recipe. Stir, then beat well or mix as directed.

Putting things right

Did your cake rise to a peak in the centre?
Use a larger tin. If still unsuccessful, place cake tin slightly lower in the oven.
Did your small buns spread too much during baking?
The mixture was too soft—add less liquid next time.
Was your cake dry?
Overcooking is the most common cause of this—try baking for a slightly shorter period.

Creaming method

Cut up the fat (softened, but not melted, in cold weather), beat until soft with a wooden spoon or spatula. Add sugar and beat until mixture is light in colour and fluffy in texture. Sieve or mix flour, salt and spice or cocoa (if used) together. Add eggs one at a time with a little of the flour mixture. Stir, then beat thoroughly. Stir in milk, syrup or honey (if included) and a little flour. Beat again. Add fruit, flavouring, etc. and remaining flour. Stir in thoroughly but do not beat. Put mixture into tin and smooth level with a palette or table knife. Bake as directed in recipe, covering cake with greaseproof paper when the top is brown enough.

Putting things right

Did your cake sink slightly in the centre?
Cream fat and sugar together slightly less. If that doesn't solve the problem, try baking the cake slightly longer next time.
Did your Victoria sandwich have large holes in it?
The remaining flour was stirred in too vigorously—use a lighter touch.
Your cake crust turned sticky on cooling?
Cream fat and sugar together more thoroughly—soften fat slightly in cold weather.

Melting method

Sieve or mix flour, salt and spices (if used). Melt fat, syrup or treacle and sugar in a saucepan over a low heat making sure you do not let them get too hot. Add melted ingredients with beaten egg and/or milk to flour and spices. Stir or beat, with a wooden spoon, until smooth as directed. Pour the mixture into the prepared tin.

Putting things right

Did your cake appear hard and dry on cutting?
A cake made by this method should be stored in a tin or wrapped in foil and left for a few days before cutting to allow it to soften.
Did your cake sink in the middle?
You added too much syrup or treacle: use a less generous spoonful.
Was your cake burnt at the edges but soggy in the centre?
This usually indicates too hot an oven.

Whisking method

Have ready a large saucepan containing 2–3 inches of boiling water and a mixing bowl which fits over the pan without touching the water. Break the eggs into the bowl, add sugar and whisk together over the boiling water until the mixture thickens and is lukewarm. Take great care not to overheat the mixture. Remove the bowl and whisk until the mixture is very thick and ropy. Add the sieved or mixed flour and salt and, using a **metal** spoon, lightly cut and fold the flour into the mixture. Do this thoroughly but **lightly** so that the air is not expelled.

If you use an electric mixer it is unnecessary to place the bowl over hot water.

Putting things right

Did your cake turn out heavy and soggy?
Either you did not beat eggs and sugar together for long enough or you did not fold in the flour *lightly* enough.
Did you find pockets of dry flour on cutting the mixture?
In which case you failed to fold the flour in *thoroughly* enough.
On rolling up your Swiss roll did it start to crack and break?
The mixture was probably overcooked, making the crust hard and dry. Alternatively, you did not roll the sponge up quickly enough after taking it from the oven and spreading with jam.

One-stage mixing

Place flour, salt, sugar, soft margarine and eggs in a bowl together with any other ingredients. Stir to blend, then beat well for about 2 minutes. Some recipes using this method include extra baking powder. This gives increased volume but causes the mixture to stale quickly.

This method is more or less infallible!

Lining a cake tin

Sandwich tin—Cake tin
Place the tin on greaseproof paper and draw round it with a pencil.

Cut just inside the pencil mark with scissors.
Cut a strip of paper long enough to go round the tin and overlap about 1 inch.
For a sandwich tin the strip should be about 2 inches deeper than the tin.

For a cake tin the strip should be about $2\frac{1}{2}$ inches deeper than the tin.

Lay the strip flat on the table and turn up $\frac{1}{2}$ inch and crease. Snip diagonally to the fold.

Brush inside the tin with melted lard or vegetable cooking fat, using a pastry brush. Insert strip so that the snipped part lies flat on the base.

Put the circle in place and lightly brush over the paper on the base and sides with fat.

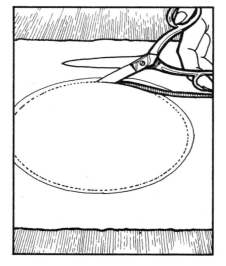

Drawing round the edge of the cake tin placed on greaseproof paper.

Cutting just inside the pencil mark with a pair of scissors.

Snipping the turned up edge of the strip diagonally to the fold.

Brushing the inside of the tin with melted fat.

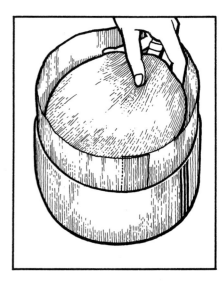

Inserting the strip so that the snipped part lies flat on the base.

Placing the circle of greaseproof paper in the bottom of the tin.

Baking times for small and large cakes

Cake	Amount	Size of tin	Oven setting	Time
Dundee, see page 47	half	5 inches round or 4 inches square	350°F., Gas mark 4 300°F., Gas mark 2	45 minutes 1 hour
	double (use half plain and half self-raising flour)	10 inches round or 9 inches square	350°F., Gas mark 4 300°F., Gas mark 2	1 hour 2 hours
Fruit cake, see page 46	half	5 inches round or 4 inches square	350°F., Gas mark 4	1 hour
	double	9 inches round or 8 inches square	350°F., Gas mark 4	2 hours
	treble	10 inches round or 9 inches square	350°F., Gas mark 4	$2\frac{1}{4}$ hours
Victoria sandwich, see page 45	normal	6 inches round or 5 inches square	350°F., Gas mark 4	50 minutes
	double	8 inches round or 7 inches square	350°F., Gas mark 4	$1\frac{1}{4}$–$1\frac{1}{2}$ hours
	5 egg	9 inches round or 8 inches square	350°F., Gas mark 4	$1\frac{1}{4}$–$1\frac{1}{2}$ hours
	6 egg	10 inches round or 9 inches square	350°F., Gas mark 4	$1\frac{1}{4}$–$1\frac{1}{2}$ hours
Christmas cake 1, see page 48	half	6 inches round or 5 inches square	350°F., Gas mark 4 275°F., Gas mark 1	45 minutes $1\frac{1}{4}$ hours
	double	10 inches round or 9 inches square	350°F., Gas mark 4 275°F., Gas mark 1	1 hour $2\frac{1}{2}$ hours
	treble	12 inches round or 11 inches square	350°F., Gas mark 4 275°F., Gas mark 1	1 hour $2\frac{3}{4}$ hours
Rich dark cake, see page 48	half	7 inches round or 6 inches square	350°F., Gas mark 4 275°F., Gas mark 1	1 hour 40 minutes
	double	11 inches round or 10 inches square	350°F., Gas mark 4 275°F., Gas mark 1	$1\frac{1}{2}$ hours $2\frac{1}{2}$ hours
Cut and come again cake, see page 46	double	8 inches round or 7 inches square	350°F., Gas mark 4	2 hours

Traditional recipes

Basic sauces

White sauce

to make ½ pint sauce:
Pouring sauce
½ oz. butter or margarine
½ oz. flour, plain or self-raising
½ pint milk
salt; pepper (or sugar)

Coating sauce
1 oz. butter or margarine
1 oz. flour, plain or self-raising
½ pint milk
salt; pepper (or sugar)

Melt fat in a saucepan, stir in flour. Cook for 1 minute over a gentle heat without browning. Gradually add the liquid, beating well after each addition. Bring to the boil, stirring all the time. Simmer for 2—3 minutes. Season to taste.

Brown sauce

to make ½ pint sauce:
½ oz. dripping, lard or cooking fat
1 small onion, peeled and chopped
1 small carrot, peeled and chopped
½ oz. flour, plain or self-raising
½ pint stock (or water and stock cube)
salt; pepper

Melt fat; add chopped vegetables and flour. Cook over a gentle heat, stirring all the time, until the mixture is a rich brown colour—take care not to burn the mixture. Blend in stock, bring to the boil, add seasoning and simmer for about 30 minutes. Strain and check seasoning.

Most traditional recipes in this country started life as regional or village specialities. Cooking depended largely on what was at hand, which meant largely what the climate, the season, the region and sometimes tradition dictated. Thus Scotland nurtured warm, filling vegetable soups, the north and lowlands became rich in scones, breads and buns—all the delights of their traditional high tea.

But communication was slow and usually confined to more important matters than cooking. Transport was even slower, and transport of perishable foodstuffs obviously unthinkable. And so for centuries the different regions developed their own specialities virtually free from outside influence. It was not until the mid-nineteenth century that those two famous cookery writers Eliza Acton and Mrs. Beeton started the ball rolling . . .

Today's farming methods, transport facilities and developments in short and long term preservation have made it possible for every housewife to cook and enjoy dishes from all over the country and the recipes which follow offer, among other things, some of the best of British traditional cooking.

Sauces

The following 6 recipes are based on the White sauce recipe, see opposite.

Cheese sauce

2—3 oz. cheese, grated
½ teaspoonful made mustard
½ pint white sauce
(pouring or coating as required)

Add cheese and mustard to the sauce and reheat thoroughly.

Parsley sauce

1 tablespoonful parsley, chopped
½ pint white sauce
(pouring or coating as required)

Add parsley to sauce just before serving.

Onion sauce

8 oz. onions, peeled and chopped
½ pint white sauce
(pouring or coating as required)

Cook onions in boiling salted water until tender; drain and add to sauce.

Cauliflower soup, page 28

Caper sauce

2-3 teaspoonfuls capers, chopped
1 teaspoonful vinegar from capers
½ pint white sauce
(pouring or coating as required)

Add capers and vinegar to sauce and reheat thoroughly.

Mustard sauce

2 teaspoonfuls dry mustard
2 teaspoonfuls vinegar
½ pint white sauce
(pouring or coating as required)

Mix mustard and vinegar to a smooth cream, add to sauce.

Egg sauce

1 egg, hardboiled and shelled
½ pint white sauce (pouring or coating as required)

Chop egg finely and add to sauce, reheat thoroughly.

Curry sauce

1 onion, peeled and chopped
1 small apple, peeled, cored and chopped
2 tablespoonfuls oil
½ oz. flour, plain or self-raising
1-2 tablespoonfuls curry powder (according to taste)
¾ pint stock
2 oz. sultanas
1 tablespoonful mango chutney
squeeze lemon juice

Fry onion and apple in oil until soft but not brown. Stir in flour and curry powder, cook gently for 1 minute. Blend in stock, sultanas, chutney and lemon juice. Bring to the boil, stirring all the time, then simmer for 30 minutes.

Quick tomato sauce

1 small onion, peeled and chopped
2 rashers bacon, de-rinded and chopped
1 tablespoonful oil
½ oz. flour, plain or self-raising
1 x 15-oz. can tomatoes
1 tablespoonful tomato purée
pinch mixed herbs
sugar
salt; pepper

Fry onion and bacon in oil until soft, but not brown. Stir in flour, cook for a few moments without browning. Add tomatoes, tomato purée, herbs and seasoning. Bring to the boil, stirring all the time, then simmer for about 15 minutes. Sieve, reheat and check seasoning.

Barbecue sauce

1 onion, peeled and chopped
1 tablespoonful oil
½ **oz.** flour, plain or self-raising
1 x 15-oz. can tomatoes
½ pint water
2 slices lemon
1 tablespoonful tomato purée
1 tablespoonful Worcestershire sauce
1 tablespoonful vinegar
pinch mixed herbs
salt; pepper
sugar

Fry onion in oil for 2 minutes, stir in flour. Blend in remaining ingredients, bring to the boil, stirring all the time, simmer for 30 minutes. Sieve, reheat and check seasoning, adding sugar to taste if you prefer a less sharp sauce.

Béchamel sauce

3 cloves
1 small onion, peeled
1 pint milk
1 bay leaf
1 small piece carrot
1 piece celery
1 oz. butter or margarine
1 oz. flour, plain or self-raising
salt; pepper

Stick cloves into onion. Place milk, onion, bay leaf, carrot and celery in a saucepan. Bring to the boil, remove from heat, cover and leave for 30 minutes. Strain and continue to make the sauce as directed in basic White sauce recipe, page 22.

Hollandaise sauce

1 egg yolk
1 tablespoonful cream
¾ pint béchamel sauce, see above
1 teaspoonful lemon juice
small pinch cayenne pepper

Mix together egg yolk and cream, add to hot sauce with lemon juice and a tiny pinch of cayenne pepper. Reheat gently without boiling.

Gravy for roast meat

to make 1 pint:
1 tablespoonful fat from roasting tin
2 tablespoonfuls flour, plain or self-raising
1 pint stock, vegetable water, or stock cube and water
salt; pepper
gravy browning (optional)

Pour off fat from the roasting tin leaving about 1 tablespoonful. Stir in flour and cook for 2-3 minutes. Gradually blend in stock or vegetable water. Bring to the boil, stirring all the time, simmer for 3 minutes. Season to taste and add gravy browning if necessary.

Mayonnaise

1 egg yolk
$\frac{1}{2}$ teaspoonful dry mustard
$\frac{1}{4}$ teaspoonful salt
$\frac{1}{4}$ teaspoonful pepper
about $\frac{1}{4}$ pint vegetable oil or olive oil
1 tablespoonful wine vinegar

Place egg yolk and seasonings in a bowl; mix well. Beat in oil, a drop at a time at first, then as mixture thickens at about 1 teaspoonful at a time. When all oil has been added, stir in vinegar and check seasoning.

If the mixture curdles, take 1 egg yolk and gradually beat in the curdled mixture, very carefully, to obtain a smooth mixture.

Blender mayonnaise

1 egg
1 teaspoonful sugar
1 teaspoonful dry mustard
$\frac{1}{2}$ teaspoonful salt
$\frac{1}{4}$ teaspoonful pepper
about $\frac{1}{2}$ pint vegetable oil or olive oil
3 tablespoonfuls wine vinegar

Place egg and seasonings in blender; mix with the lid on for a few seconds. Set the blender at a low speed, remove centre cap of lid and slowly pour in some of the oil in a thin stream until the mixture thickens. Add remaining oil more quickly. Add vinegar and check seasoning.

Soufflés

Savoury soufflés

1 oz. butter or margarine
1 oz. flour, plain or self-raising
$\frac{1}{4}$ pint milk
salt; pepper
3 eggs, separated
chosen filling (see below)

Grease a 7-inch soufflé dish or deep ovenproof dish. Make a sauce with the fat, flour and milk, see page 22. Remove from the heat, add seasoning to taste, egg yolks and chosen filling (see below), beat well. Whisk egg whites until stiff.
Stir 2 tablespoonfuls egg white into the mixture then fold in remainder.
Put mixture in to the dish and bake for 35 minutes at 400°F., Gas mark 6. Serve immediately.

Fillings for savoury soufflés

Ham
3 oz. cooked ham, finely chopped, with a pinch cayenne pepper.

Fish
3 oz. cooked smoked haddock or cod, finely pounded and $\frac{1}{2}$ teaspoontul anchovy essence.

Cheese
Use only $\frac{1}{2}$ oz. flour in the basic sauce, add 3 oz. cheese, grated, and $\frac{1}{2}$ teaspoonful dry mustard.

Onion and mushroom
Fry 1 small onion, peeled and grated, in the fat before making the sauce. Add 4 oz. mushrooms, finely chopped and fried in $\frac{1}{2}$ oz. butter.

Sweet soufflés

1 oz. butter or margarine
1 oz. flour, plain or self-raising
$\frac{1}{4}$ pint milk
1 oz. caster sugar
3 egg yolks
4 egg whites
chosen flavouring (see below)

Prepare and bake at 400°F., Gas mark 6, as for Savoury soufflés, see page 25, using caster sugar instead of salt and pepper.

Flavourings for sweet soufflés

Coffee
Dissolve 2 tablespoonfuls instant coffee in the milk before making the sauce.

Chocolate
Dissolve 2 oz. plain chocolate, grated, in the milk before making the sauce, add $\frac{1}{2}$ teaspoonful vanilla essence.

Orange or lemon
Add finely grated rind and juice of 1 orange or 1 lemon to the sauce after cooking.

Vanilla
Add 2 teaspoonfuls vanilla essence to the sauce after cooking.

Soups

Tomato soup

$\frac{1}{2}$ **oz.** butter or margarine
1 onion, peeled and chopped
1 carrot, peeled and chopped
1 stick celery, sliced
1 rasher bacon, de-rinded and diced
$\frac{1}{2}$ **oz.** flour, plain or self-raising
1 x 1$\frac{1}{4}$-lb. can tomatoes
$\frac{3}{4}$ pint stock
1 tablespoonful tomato purée
salt; pepper
sugar
pinch mixed herbs

Heat fat and fry vegetables and bacon for 5 minutes without browning. Stir in flour and add remaining ingredients. Bring to the boil, stirring all the time. Simmer gently for 45 minutes. Sieve or liquidise and return to the saucepan. Check seasoning before serving.

Opposite: Ingredients for making mayonnaise, page 25
Below: Tomato soup

Cream of vegetable soup

1 oz. butter or margarine
chosen vegetables (see below), prepared
1 oz. flour, plain or self-raising
1½ pints stock (or water and stock cubes)
1 egg yolk
¼ pint milk
salt; pepper
parsley

Melt the butter, add the prepared vegetables and cook gently for 5 minutes without browning. Stir in the flour, cook for 1 minute then blend in the stock. Simmer until the vegetables are tender. Sieve or liquidise and return to the saucepan. Blend the egg yolk and milk. Add to the soup and reheat gently without boiling; check seasoning.
Sprinkle with chopped parsley and if liked serve with croûtons.

Vegetables to use

Cauliflower
1 medium cauliflower, trimmed and broken into
  sprigs
1 medium onion, peeled and chopped

Leeks
1 lb. leeks

Cut off the coarse dark green tops of leeks, split in 2 lengthwise and clean thoroughly; slice.

Onions
1 lb. onions, peeled and sliced into rings

Celery
1 medium head of celery
1 medium onion, peeled and chopped

Cut off root and larger leaves of celery (the small leaves may be added to the soup), divide into stalks and wash thoroughly; slice.

Carrots
12 oz. carrots, peeled and sliced
1 small onion, peeled and chopped
2 stalks celery, sliced

Mushrooms
8 oz. mushrooms, washed and sliced
1 small onion, peeled and chopped

Mixed vegetables
1 lb. mixed vegetables—onions, carrots, celery and
  turnips

Wash, prepare and slice the vegetables.

Kidney soup

1 onion, peeled and chopped
8 oz. ox kidney, finely diced
1 tablespoonful oil
½ **oz.** flour, plain or self-raising
1½ pints beef stock
1 tablespoonful tomato purée
salt; pepper
1 tablespoonful medium or sweet sherry

Fry onion and kidney in oil until brown. Stir in flour; cook for 1 minute. Blend in stock and tomato purée. Simmer until the kidney is tender (about 1 hour). Check seasoning; add sherry just before serving.

Mulligatawny soup

1 tablespoonful oil
½ **oz.** butter or margarine
1 carrot, peeled and sliced
1 onion, peeled and chopped
1 small cooking apple, peeled, cored and chopped
1 oz. flour, plain or self-raising
1 tablespoonful curry powder (or more according to
  taste)
1½ pints stock
2½ fl. oz. milk
salt; pepper

Heat oil and butter; gently fry the prepared vegetables and apple until soft. Stir in the flour and curry powder, cook for 1 minute. Blend in the stock, simmer for 30 minutes. Sieve or liquidise, return to the saucepan. Add the milk and reheat. Check seasoning.

Pastry dishes: savoury

Cheese tartlets

shortcrust pastry using 4 oz. flour etc., see page 16

Filling:
1 oz. butter or margarine
1 oz. flour, plain or self-raising
¼ pint milk
2 oz. cheese, grated
1 egg, separated
salt; pepper

Line 12 greased tartlet or bun tins with rolled out pastry. Make a sauce with the fat, flour and milk, see page 22. Remove from heat, stir in cheese and egg yolk; season to taste. Fold in the stiffly beaten egg white and divide mixture between the pastry cases. Bake for 20 minutes at 400°F., Gas mark 6.

Bacon roll

suet pastry using 8 oz. flour etc., see page 16

Filling:
8 oz. bacon rashers, de-rinded
1 small onion, peeled and chopped
2 tomatoes, skinned and sliced
4 oz. mushrooms
1 tablespoonful parsley, chopped
pepper
a little beaten egg

Roll out pastry to a rectangle approximately 16 by 10 inches.
Lay the bacon rashers over the pastry, cover with the onion, tomatoes, mushrooms and parsley.
Sprinkle with pepper; brush edges with beaten egg.
Roll up loosely, starting at the short end and sealing well at the join and edges.
Place on a greased baking tray, with the join underneath. Bake for 35 minutes at 400°F., Gas mark 6.

Sausage rolls

flaky pastry using 8 oz. flour etc., see page 16

1 lb. sausages or sausagemeat
a little beaten egg

Remove sausage skins and make sausages into 2 x 14-inch rolls—flour the table or pastry board to make this easier.
Roll out pastry to an oblong about the same length as the sausages, cut in 2 lengthways.
Brush edges of pastry with beaten egg and place a sausage roll on each strip.
Fold pastry over and seal edge firmly, knock up with the back of a knife.
Cut each roll into 6, make 2 little slits in each sausage roll and brush with beaten egg.
Place on an ungreased baking tray and bake for 20 minutes at 450°F., Gas mark 8.

Savoury flans

shortcrust pastry using 6 oz. flour etc., see page 16

2 large eggs, beaten
½ small can evaporated milk
salt; pepper
filling (see opposite)

Roll out pastry and line a greased 8-inch flan ring.
Mix together eggs, milk and seasoning.
Arrange chosen filling in pastry case, pour over egg mixture. Bake for 30-35 minutes at 375°F., Gas mark 5.

Fillings for savoury flans

Chicken and sweetcorn
6 oz. chicken, cooked and diced
1 x 7-oz. can sweetcorn, drained

Shrimp and cheese
1 x 4-oz. can shrimps, drained
3 oz. cheese, grated

Bacon and pineapple
4 oz. bacon, diced and fried
1 x 8-oz. can pineapple rings, drained

Crab and asparagus
1 x 3½-oz. can crabmeat
1 x 10-oz. can asparagus spears, drained

Onion and chicken liver
8 oz. chicken livers, chopped and fried
1 onion, cut in rings and fried

Bacon and egg pie

shortcrust pastry using 6 oz. flour etc., see page 16

Filling:
8 oz. streaky bacon, chopped
3 eggs
pepper
a little beaten egg

Roll out two-thirds of pastry to line a 7-inch sandwich tin.
Place bacon into pastry case and arrange it so that there are 3 hollows for the eggs.
Drop an egg into each hollow, sprinkle with pepper.
Roll out the remaining pastry for a lid, using a little beaten egg to seal the edges.
Make 'leaves' from the pastry trimmings, if liked, for decoration. Brush the pie with beaten egg and bake for 35 minutes at 400°F., Gas mark 6.

Smoked fish turnover

flaky or shortcrust pastry using 8 oz. flour etc., see page 16

Filling:
¾ **oz.** butter or margarine
¾ **oz.** flour, plain or self-raising
¼ pint milk
salt; pepper
pinch ground nutmeg
1 teaspoonful parsley, chopped
1 egg, hardboiled and chopped
3 tablespoonfuls potato, cooked and mashed
8 oz. smoked fish, cooked and flaked
a little beaten egg

Make a sauce with the fat, flour and milk, see page 22. Season to taste. Stir in remaining ingredients and put aside to cool. Roll out pastry thinly into a square, trim the edges. Place the filling in the centre of the pastry, brush the edges with beaten egg. Fold the 4 corners into the centre like an envelope, seal edges well together. Brush with beaten egg and bake for 40 minutes at 400°F., Gas mark 6.

Steak and kidney pie

flaky or rough puff pastry using 8 oz. flour etc., see pages 16 and 18

Filling:
1 oz. flour, plain or self-raising
salt; pepper
1½ **lb.** chuck steak, cubed
4 oz. ox kidney, chopped
1 oz. cooking fat
stock or water

Mix the flour with a little salt and pepper, toss the meat and kidney in the flour. Brown in hot fat, stir in 1 pint stock or water. Bring to the boil and simmer until the meat is tender, 1–1¾ hours. Pour into a 2-pint pie dish, cool.
Roll out the pastry to an oblong about 2 inches larger than top of pie dish. Place pie dish in the centre of the pastry and cut round it to obtain an oval of pastry the same size as the top of the dish; put to one side.
Cut a strip about ½ inch wide, damp the edge of the pie dish and place the strip round the edge; damp the strip.
Place the pastry 'lid' on top, seal the edge firmly and trim neatly. Knock up and flute the edges with the back of a knife to give a layered effect. Make a small hole in the centre of the pastry lid and decorate pastry with 'leaves' made from pastry trimmings rolled out

and cut first into a long strip ¾–1 inch wide, then into 4 or 5 diamond-shaped pieces, each with 'veins' marked on with a knife.
Brush top of pie with beaten egg and bake for 30 minutes at 425°F., Gas mark 7, covering top with greaseproof paper when brown enough.

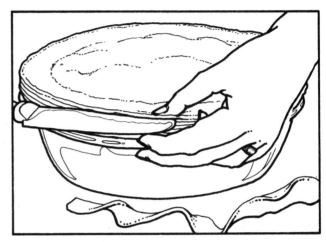

Knocking up the pastry edge with the back of a knife to give a layered effect.

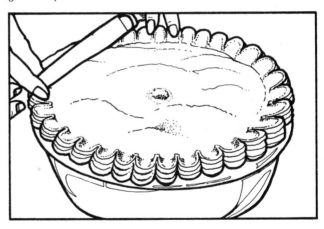

Fluting the pastry edge to give an attractive finish.

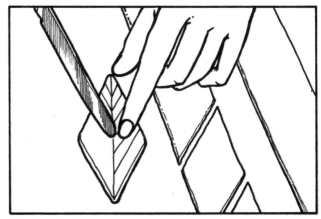

Marking 'veins' with a knife in the diamond-shaped pieces of pastry trimmings.

Cheese soufflé, page 25

Steak and kidney pudding

suet pastry using 8 oz. self-raising flour etc., see page 16

Filling:
1 oz. flour, plain or self-raising
salt; pepper
12 oz. chuck steak, cubed
4 oz. ox kidney, chopped
stock or water

Grease a 2-pint pudding basin. Prepare pastry and roll out two-thirds to line the basin; roll out remainder to make a lid. Mix the flour with a little salt and pepper. Toss the steak and kidney in the flour and put into the lined basin. Add stock or water until basin is three-quarters full. Place 'lid' on top, sealing edges well with cold water. Cover with greased foil or greaseproof paper and steam for 4 hours.

Lamb and apricot pudding

Filling:
12 oz. lean lamb, cubed
1 oz. flour
salt; pepper
4 oz. dried apricots
chicken stock or water

Make as for Steak and kidney pudding using 8 oz. suet pastry etc.; steam for $3\frac{1}{2}$ hours.

Beef and tomato pudding

Filling:
1 lb. lean mince
1 oz. flour
1 x 8-oz. can tomatoes
$\frac{1}{2}$ teaspoonful mixed herbs

Make as for Steak and kidney pudding using 8 oz. suet pastry etc. Mix the tomatoes and herbs with the meat; steam for 3 hours.

Pork and apple pudding

Filling:
12 oz. lean pork, cubed
1 oz. flour
1 large cooking apple, peeled, cored and diced
chicken stock or water

Make as for Steak and kidney pudding using 8 oz. suet pastry etc. Mix the apple with the meat; steam for 4 hours.

Pastry dishes: sweet

Fruit tart

shortcrust pastry using 8 oz. flour etc., see page 16

Filling:
1$\frac{1}{2}$ lb. fruit in season (apples, plums, gooseberries, for example)
sugar

Place a baking tray into the oven while making the tart. Grease an 8-inch ovenproof plate. Cut pastry into 2 pieces, one slightly larger than the other. Roll out the smaller piece and line the pie plate, trim the edge. Fill with half of the prepared fruit, sprinkle with sugar and cover with remaining fruit; damp the edge. Roll out remaining pastry and cover tart with it. Seal edges well and trim neatly.
Make a small hole in the centre, brush surface with milk or egg white and sprinkle with caster sugar; place on the preheated baking tray. Bake for at least 30 minutes or until the fruit is tender at 375°F., Gas mark 5, covering with greaseproof paper when top is brown enough.

Rich Bakewell tart

shortcrust using 4 oz. flour etc., see page 16

Filling:
2 tablespoonfuls apricot jam
2 oz. mixed peel (optional)
2 oz. butter or margarine
2 oz. caster sugar
$\frac{1}{2}$ **oz.** self-raising flour
1 egg
2 oz. ground almonds
few drops almond essence
1 oz. almonds, split and blanched

Grease a 7-inch flan ring or sandwich tin and line with the pastry. Spread with apricot jam and sprinkle with the mixed peel, if used. Prepare the mixture by the creaming method, see page 19, and spread evenly into the pastry case. Bake for 10 minutes at 375°F., Gas mark 5, then scatter over the almonds and bake for a further 20 minutes.

Sausage rolls, page 29; bacon and egg pie, page 29; cream buns, page 37

Apple tart, page 32

Lemon meringue pie

shortcrust pastry using 6 oz. flour etc., see page 16

Filling:
2 lemons
1½ oz. cornflour
½ pint water
2 egg yolks
3 oz. caster sugar

Meringue:
2 egg whites
4 oz. caster sugar

Grease an 8-inch flan ring or sandwich tin and line with the pastry. Bake 'blind', see page 16, for 15 minutes at 400°F., Gas mark 6; remove foil and return to oven for 3–5 minutes.
Meanwhile prepare the filling: blend the cornflour with a little water to a smooth cream. Heat the remaining water, grated lemon rind and juice, stir in the cornflour and bring to the boil stirring all the time. Cook for 2 minutes, remove from the heat. Stir in the sugar and egg yolks: cool before pouring into the pastry case.
Whisk the egg whites until very stiff, whisk in half of the sugar a little at a time, then fold in the remainder. Spread over the lemon filling, right to the edge and swirl attractively. Bake for a further 35–40 minutes at 300°F., Gas mark 2, to crisp the meringue.

Dutch apple tart

shortcrust pastry using 8 oz. flour etc., see page 16

Filling:
1¼ lb. cooking apples, prepared and sliced
4 oz. soft brown sugar
1 teaspoonful cinnamon
¼ teaspoonful ground nutmeg
2 oz. sultanas
2 oz. blanched almonds, chopped
½ **oz.** butter or margarine

Follow the directions for Fruit tart, see page 32, using above filling as follows: mix together the sugar, spices, sultanas and almonds. Place half the apples on to the pastry-lined plate, cover with the sugar mixture, then the remaining apples.

Mince pies

to make about 12:
shortcrust pastry using 8 oz. flour etc., see page 16

mincemeat
caster sugar

Roll out pastry to just under ¼ inch thick, cut out rounds, half of them slightly larger than the patty tins to be used, the remainder the same size as the patty tins, for use as 'lids'. Line the greased patty tins and place a little mincemeat in each. Damp the edges of the 'lids' and seal the edges firmly. Re-roll the trimmings and cut out more rounds. Bake for 15 minutes at 400°F., Gas mark 6, then remove from the oven, brush with water and sprinkle with caster sugar, return to oven for 5 minutes.

Almond slices

shortcrust or flan pastry using 6 oz. flour etc., see page 16

Filling:
jam
2 egg whites
2 oz. ground almonds
3 oz. icing sugar, sieved
few drops almond essence
3 oz. blanched almonds, chopped

Grease a Swiss roll tin 11 by 8 inches and line with the pastry; spread thinly with jam. Whisk egg whites until stiff, stir in the ground almonds, sugar and essence. Spread mixture evenly over the jam and sprinkle with chopped almonds. Bake for 25 minutes at 375°F., Gas mark 5. Trim edges and cut into fingers while warm. Substitute 2 oz. desiccated coconut for ground almonds if preferred.

Syrup oat slices

shortcrust pastry using 6 oz. flour etc., see page 16

Filling:
apricot jam
3 tablespoonfuls warmed golden syrup
3 oz. butter or margarine
few drops almond essence
6 tablespoonfuls porage oats
6 tablespoonfuls desiccated coconut

Grease a Swiss roll tin 11 by 7 inches. Line it with the pastry and spread with apricot jam. Warm syrup and fat until fat melts, stir in almond essence, oats and coconut. Spread over jam and bake for 20 minutes at 375°F., Gas mark 5. Trim the edges and cut into fingers while warm.

Eccles cakes

flaky pastry using 8 oz. flour etc., see page 16

Filling:
1 oz. butter
8 oz. currants
3 oz. soft brown sugar
1 oz. cut mixed peel
½ teaspoonful mixed spice
caster sugar

Roll out the pastry just under ¼ inch thick; cut into rounds with a small saucer or large scone cutter. Mix together the ingredients for the filling, turn over the pastry rounds and put a little filling in the centre of each. Brush the edge with water and gather into the centre pressing firmly together. Turn over and roll until the currants begin to show. Make 2 small cuts on top, brush with water and sprinkle with caster sugar. Bake for 20 minutes at 425°F., Gas mark 7.

Cream horns

trimmings of flaky or rough puff pastry
egg white

To finish:
jam; whipped cream

Place trimmings neatly one on top of the other and roll out thinly. Cut into 1-inch wide strips, brush lightly with beaten egg white. Grease some cream horn tins and, starting at the pointed end, wind the pastry round overlapping each layer with the un-glazed side next to the tin. The pastry should not overlap the open end. Lay the covered tins, short side down, on wetted baking sheets and put aside in a cold place for 30 minutes before baking. Brush with egg white and bake for 10 minutes at 450°F., Gas mark 8. Carefully remove the moulds and return the pastry to the oven for 5 minutes. When cool, place a little jam in each and fill with whipped cream.

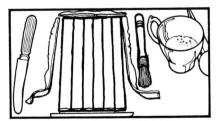

Cutting the thinly rolled out pastry into 1-inch wide strips.

Brushing the cream horn tins with melted fat.

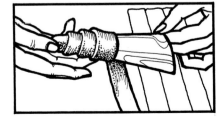

Winding the pastry round the horn tins, starting at the pointed end, and overlapping each layer.

Cream buns

half-quantity choux pastry, see page 18, omitting the caster sugar

whipped cream
icing sugar

Grease the bottoms of 2 large cake tins and place teaspoonfuls of pastry 2 inches apart in the tins. Cover tins with foil and place in the oven, one above and one below the centre. Bake covered for 20 minutes at 425°F., Gas mark 7, then reverse the tins, still covered, for the remaining 20 minutes. Split the buns in 2 while hot. When cool fill with a little whipped cream and dust with icing sugar.

Chocolate éclairs

choux pastry using 4 oz. flour etc., see page 18

whipped cream
chocolate glacé icing, see page 51

Place pastry into a piping bag fitted with $\frac{5}{8}$-inch diameter plain tube. Pipe in 3-inch lengths on greased baking sheets, cutting the mixture off sharply with a knife dipped in hot water and allowing space for the éclairs to expand. Cook for 30 minutes at 375°F., Gas mark 5, on the shelf above the middle. Split while hot and scoop out the soft centres. When cool, fill pastry cases with whipped cream and ice with chocolate glacé icing.

Puddings

Steamed sponge pudding

3 oz. butter or margarine
3 oz. caster sugar
5 oz. self-raising flour
pinch salt
2 eggs
1 tablespoonful milk

Prepare the mixture by the creaming or one-stage method, see pages 19 and 20. Place the mixture into a greased 1½-pint pudding basin and cover closely with greased foil or greaseproof paper. Steam or boil for 1½ hours. Serve with custard or a sauce (see opposite).

Jam cap pudding

Jam cap pudding or syrup pudding

Place 2–3 tablespoonfuls jam or golden syrup in the basin and place the sponge mixture on top. Steam or boil in the usual way.

Chocolate pudding

Use 1 oz. cocoa in place of 1 oz. flour. Sieve together the flour, salt and cocoa. Add a few drops of vanilla essence and steam or boil in the usual way.

Orange or lemon pudding

Add the grated rind of 1 orange or 1 lemon to the mixture and steam or boil in the usual way.

Sauces to serve with steamed puddings

Apricot or raspberry jam sauce

Heat 6 oz. jam with 2 tablespoonfuls water and a squeeze of lemon juice. Sieve if a smoother sauce is required.

Chocolate sauce

2 oz. cocoa
4 oz. soft brown sugar
½ pint milk
a few drops vanilla essence

Mix together cocoa and sugar in a small saucepan. Blend in milk and essence. Bring to the boil, stirring all the time, simmer for 2 minutes. Add the essence and serve hot or cold.

Vanilla sauce

½ pint white pouring sauce, see page 22
1 tablespoonful sugar
½ teaspoonful vanilla essence

Add sugar and essence to the sauce after cooking.

Orange sauce

4 teaspoonfuls cornflour
½ pint water
grated rind ½ orange
juice 1 orange
juice ½ lemon
2 tablespoonfuls granulated sugar

Blend cornflour with a little cold water, boil remainder with rind and juice. Pour on to blended cornflour, return to saucepan. Reboil 2–3 minutes, sweeten to taste and serve.

Lemon pudding

suet pastry using 8 oz. self-raising flour etc., see page 16

1 lemon
8 oz. demerara sugar
1 oz. butter

Grease a 2-pint pudding basin. Roll out two-thirds of the pastry to line the basin, roll out the remaining piece for a lid. Grate lemon rind, peel off the white pith and chop the flesh, mix lemon rind and flesh with the sugar and butter, cut in small pieces. Place filling in basin and put on 'lid' sealing the edges firmly with a little cold water. Cover with greased foil or greaseproof paper and steam for 3 hours.
Serve with custard or a sauce.

Christmas pudding

to make either 4 puddings in $\frac{3}{4}$-pint basins; 1 in a $2\frac{1}{2}$-pint basin + 1 in a $1\frac{1}{4}$-pint basin; or 3 in $1\frac{1}{4}$-pint basins:

8 oz. self-raising flour
$\frac{1}{2}$ teaspoonful salt
1 teaspoonful ground cinnamon
1 teaspoonful ground nutmeg
1 teaspoonful mixed spice
8 oz. breadcrumbs
8 oz. shredded suet
juice and rind 1 lemon
8 oz. raisins
8 oz. currants
8 oz. sultanas
4 oz. mixed peel
6 oz. demerara sugar
1 cooking apple, peeled and chopped
4 eggs, beaten
$2\frac{1}{2}$ **fl. oz.** brandy
$7\frac{1}{2}$ **fl. oz.** milk, stout or ale

Sieve flour, salt and spices, mix in the breadcrumbs and suet. Clean the dried fruit if necessary. Add remaining dry ingredients, then the eggs and liquid. Mix well and place in greased basins, filling to within $\frac{1}{2}$ inch of the top. Cover with greased greaseproof paper and foil or a pudding cloth. Place puddings in saucepan, pour boiling water round basins until water comes two-thirds up the sides. Boil the puddings for 8 hours, replenishing water as necessary. Alternatively steam for 10 hours. When cool, remove the coverings and replace with fresh ones. Store in a cool dry place.

When puddings are required boil or steam for a further 2—3 hours. Serve with brandy or rum butter.

Brandy or rum butter

4 oz. butter (preferably unsalted)
4 oz. soft brown sugar
brandy or rum to taste

Cream butter until soft; add sugar. Beat until light and fluffy. Add brandy or rum to taste.

Eve's pudding

1 lb. cooking apples
2 oz. sugar
2 oz. butter or margarine
2 oz. caster sugar
3 oz. self-raising flour
pinch salt
1 egg
1 tablespoonful milk

Prepare the apples and slice, put in a 2-pint pie dish with the sugar. Make the sponge by the creaming method, see page 19, and spread over the apples. Bake for 35—40 minutes, 375°F., Gas mark 5, covering with greaseproof paper when brown.

Ginger upsidedown pudding

1 x 15-oz. can pears
2 oz. soft brown sugar
4 oz. self-raising flour
pinch salt
1 teaspoonful ground ginger
3 oz. butter or margarine
2 oz. caster sugar
1 tablespoonful black treacle
1 egg
3 tablespoonfuls milk

Drain the pears, place 2 tablespoonfuls juice in a well greased 8-inch sandwich tin and sprinkle with the soft brown sugar. Arrange the pears on the sugar, cut side down. Prepare the mixture by the creaming method, see page 19, adding the treacle to the fat and caster sugar. Spread mixture over the pears and bake for 30 minutes at 375°F., Gas mark 5. Invert on to a warmed serving plate. Serve with cream or ice-cream.

Opposite: Ginger upsidedown pudding
Below: Strawberry sponge flan

Sponge flan

4 oz. butter or margarine
4 oz. caster sugar
4 oz. self-raising flour
pinch salt
2 eggs

Filling:
fresh fruit, cleaned and prepared or canned fruit, drained

Glaze:
2 tablespoonfuls jam (raspberry or apricot depending on fruit used for filling)
squeeze lemon juice

Grease an 8½-inch sponge flan tin, cut a small circle of greaseproof paper and place in the centre of the tin. Prepare mixture by the creaming or one-stage method, see pages 19 and 20, spread evenly into the prepared flan tin and bake for 20 minutes at 375°F., Gas mark 5. When cool, fill flan with fruit, heat jam and lemon juice together to make glaze and brush or spoon over fruit while hot. Serve with cream.

Baked alaska

1 baked sponge flan case (see preceding recipe)
1 x 15-oz. can fruit cocktail
1 family-size block ice cream
3 egg whites
6 oz. caster sugar

Place flan case on a large ovenproof plate or a baking tray covered with foil. Drain fruit cocktail and arrange in flan case. Place ice cream on top, trimming the corners if necessary. Whisk the egg whites until very stiff. Whisk in 2 tablespoonfuls sugar, then fold in remainder. Spoon over the entire flan and swirl with a knife. 'Flash-bake' for 3 minutes in a very hot oven, 450°F., Gas mark 8.

Steamed fruit pudding

suet pastry using 8 oz. self-raising flour etc., see page 16

Filling:
1½ lb. fruit (apples, plums, for example)
4 oz. sugar
2 tablespoonfuls water

Prepare the fruit according to type and cut into pieces if necessary. Mix with the sugar and water. Make the pudding as for Steak and kidney pudding, see page 31, steam for 2 hours. Turn out and serve with cream or custard.

Pineapple pudding

1½ oz. butter or margarine
1 x 15-oz. can pineapple, drained and chopped, reserving juice
1½ oz. flour, plain or self-raising
pinch salt
¾ pint milk
2 oz. caster sugar
2 egg yolks

Meringue:
2 egg whites
4 oz. caster sugar

Melt the fat, stir in the flour and salt. Cook for a few seconds, then add the juice from the pineapple. Mix well then gradually blend in the milk. Bring to the boil, stirring all the time and simmer for 2 minutes. Stir in the 2 oz. caster sugar, egg yolks and pineapple and pour into a greased 2-pint pie dish.

To make meringue: whisk the egg whites until stiff and gradually whisk in the 4 oz. caster sugar. Pile on top of the pineapple mixture and bake for 30 minutes at 300°F., Gas mark 2, until crisp and pale golden.

Toffee sponge pudding

Sponge:
4 oz. self-raising flour
4 oz. soft margarine
4 oz. caster sugar
2 eggs
½ teaspoonful vanilla essence

Sauce:
1 oz. butter or margarine
4 oz. soft dark brown sugar
¼ pint water
½ oz. cornflour + 2 tablespoonfuls water to mix

Prepare the sponge mixture by the one-stage method, see page 20. Transfer to a deep ovenproof dish. Melt butter, add sugar and water, stir until sugar is dissolved. Blend cornflour with 2 tablespoonfuls water and pour into sugar syrup. Bring to the boil stirring well. Pour over the sponge and bake for 40 minutes at 375°F., Gas mark 5.

Toffee sponge pudding

Chocolate fudge pudding

Sponge:
4 oz. butter or margarine
4 oz. caster sugar
5 oz. self-raising flour
pinch salt
¾ oz. cocoa
2 eggs
1 tablespoonful milk
½ teaspoonful vanilla essence

Topping:
4 tablespoonfuls cocoa
4 oz. soft brown sugar
1 oz. butter or margarine
⅓ pint hot water

Grease a 3-pint casserole dish. Prepare sponge mixture by the creaming method, see page 19. Spread mixture evenly in the casserole. Sprinkle the sieved cocoa and brown sugar evenly over the surface, dot with butter or margarine, pour over the hot water. Bake for 45 minutes at 350°F., Gas mark 4.
Cover the top of the pudding with greaseproof paper to prevent it from becoming too brown.

Fruit crumble

1 lb. fruit (apples, gooseberries or plums, for example)
sugar (about **2–4 oz.** according to fruit)
water (1–2 tablespoonfuls as necessary)

Crumble:
4 oz. flour, plain or self-raising
pinch salt
2 oz. butter or margarine
1½ oz. granulated sugar

Prepare fruit and place in a greased 1½-pint pie dish. Stir in sugar and add a little water. Put into preheated oven on a baking tray while preparing the crumble: mix flour and salt; rub in the fat and stir in granulated sugar. Sprinkle over the fruit and bake for 25–30 minutes at 375°F., Gas mark 5.

Batters

Yorkshire pudding

4 oz. plain flour*
good pinch salt
1 egg + ½ pint milk (or milk and water mixed) or
    2 eggs + **8¾ fl. oz.** milk
about **1 oz.** dripping,
    lard or cooking fat

Place fat in a shallow tin, approximately 9 by 6 inches, and put into the oven to heat. Mix flour and salt, make a well in the centre of mixture and drop in the egg(s) and a little milk. Mix in the flour stirring to keep the mixture smooth and gradually adding half the milk. Beat well, then stir in remaining milk. When the fat is smoking hot, pour in the batter and bake for 30–35 minutes at 425°F., Gas mark 7, second shelf down from top.
*Strong plain flour is best for Yorkshire pudding.

To make individual puddings, use half-quantity batter, divide between 9–10 bun tins which have been preheated in oven with a little fat in each tin. Bake 15–20 minutes.

Pancakes

Yorkshire pudding batter using 4 oz. plain flour etc., see above

a little fat or oil for frying

Pour batter into a jug. Heat a little fat or oil in a frying pan about 6–7 inches in diameter. Pour in a little batter (just enough to cover the bottom) and quickly tilt the pan around to spread the batter thinly over the base. Cook until brown then turn over and brown on other side. Sprinkle with lemon juice and caster sugar or spread with one of the suggested fillings, see below, and roll up.

Sweet fillings for pancakes

Dutch apple
1 lb. cooking apples
2 oz. sultanas
¼ teaspoonful cinnamon
sugar to taste

Cook the prepared apples with the sultanas in a little water until soft. Add the cinnamon and sugar to taste.

Cherry almond

1 x 15-oz. can stoned cherries
4 teaspoonfuls cornflour
1 oz. blanched almonds, chopped
few drops almond essence

Place cherries into a small saucepan, heat gently. Blend cornflour to a smooth cream with a little cherry juice, stir into the cherries and bring mixture to the boil, stirring all the time. Cook for 1 minute then stir in the almonds and almond essence.

Golden raisin

6 oz. raisins
2 tablespoonfuls golden syrup
juice ½ lemon

Heat all the ingredients gently together.

Pear and ginger

1 x 15-oz. can pears, drained
1 tablespoonful stem ginger, chopped
pinch ground ginger

Dice pears and mix with ginger. Add a little pear juice and syrup from the stem ginger to moisten. Heat all the ingredients gently together.

Honey banana

3–4 bananas, thickly sliced
2 tablespoonfuls clear honey
juice ½ lemon

Heat all the ingredients gently together.

Fruit fritters

4 oz. plain flour
pinch salt
¼ pint water
1 tablespoonful oil
fresh or canned fruit
fat or oil for deep frying

Mix flour and salt, gradually beat in the water, stir in the tablespoonful of oil. Prepare the fruit as necessary (see below). Dip the pieces of prepared fruit into the batter using a fork. Fry in hot, deep fat or oil for about 5–8 minutes until golden brown and crisp. Drain on absorbent paper.

Fresh: Peel, core and slice apples; peel and halve small firm bananas; peel, core and slice small ripe pears; peel and core rings of pineapple.
Canned: Use well drained canned pineapple rings, peach halves or pears.

Cakes and buns

Queen cakes

4 oz. butter or margarine
4 oz. caster sugar
6 oz. self-raising flour
pinch salt
2 eggs
2 tablespoonfuls milk
4 oz. currants

Prepare mixture by the creaming or one-stage method, see pages 19 and 20. Divide mixture evenly between 18–20 paper baking cases or greased bun tins. Bake for 15–20 minutes at 375°F., Gas mark 5.

Iced cherry cakes

Ingredients as for Queen cakes (see above), substituting 4 oz. glacé cherries, chopped, for the currants. Toss the cherries in a little of the weighed flour before adding to the mixture. Divide mixture between 18–20 paper baking cases. Bake for 15–20 minutes at 375°F., Gas mark 5. When the cakes are cool, ice with white or pink glacé icing, using 10 oz. icing sugar etc., see page 51. Top each cake with half a glacé cherry.

Fairy fruit cakes

3 oz. butter or margarine
3 oz. caster sugar
4 oz. self-raising flour
pinch salt
1 egg
2 tablespoonfuls milk
2 oz. currants
1 oz. glacé cherries, chopped, or **1 oz.** mixed peel
grated rind ½ orange or ½ teaspoonful mixed spice

Prepare mixture by the creaming or one-stage method, see pages 19 and 20. Divide the mixture between 14–16 paper baking cases or greased patty tins. Bake for 15–20 minutes at 375°F., Gas mark 5.

Iced pineapple cakes

2 oz. butter or margarine
2 oz. caster sugar
2 oz. self-raising flour
pinch salt
1 egg
3 oz. canned pineapple, drained and chopped

Prepare mixture by creaming or one-stage method, see pages 19 and 20, adding the pineapple with the flour. Divide the mixture between 10 paper baking cases. Bake for 15—20 minutes at 375 °F., Gas mark 5. When the cakes are cool, ice with white or yellow glacé icing, using 5 oz. icing sugar etc., see page 51.

Iced honey cakes

2 oz. butter or margarine
2 tablespoonfuls honey
3 oz. self-raising flour
pinch salt
1 egg
2 oz. cherries, chopped

Prepare mixture by the creaming method (creaming fat and honey), see page 19. Divide the mixture between 10 paper baking cases. Bake for 15—20 minutes at 375 °F., Gas mark 5. When the cakes are cool, ice with white glacé icing, using 5 oz. icing sugar etc., see page 51.

Chocolate cakes

4 oz. self-raising flour
pinch salt
1 oz. drinking chocolate
1 teaspoonful cocoa
2 oz. butter or margarine
2 oz. caster sugar
1 egg
3 tablespoonfuls milk
few drops vanilla essence

Prepare mixture by the rubbing-in method, see page 19. Divide mixture between 12—14 paper baking cases or greased bun tins. Bake for 15—20 minutes at 375 °F., Gas mark 5.

To make butterflies, cut a thin slice from the top of each cake when cool, cut each slice in half. Spread or pipe a little vanilla butter cream, see page 50, on each cake and replace the 2 halves to represent wings. For plain butterflies, omit drinking chocolate and cocoa and use 5 oz. flour.

Fairy fruit cakes, opposite; cherry cake, page 47

Viennese rosettes

8 oz. butter or margarine
3 oz. icing sugar, sieved
8 oz. self-raising flour; pinch salt

Beat the fat and icing sugar in a warmed bowl until very soft. This is very important, otherwise the mixture will be too stiff to pipe. Stir in the flour and salt. Put into a forcing bag fitted with a large star nozzle and pipe large rosettes into 16–18 paper baking cases. Bake for about 20 minutes at 350°F., Gas mark 4. When cool, dust with sieved icing sugar and put a little red jam in the centre of each.

Honey buns

8 oz. self-raising flour
pinch salt
3 oz. butter or margarine
1 oz. caster sugar
2 tablespoonfuls clear honey
1 egg
2 tablespoonfuls milk

Prepare mixture by the rubbing-in method, see page 19. Divide the mixture between 18–20 paper baking cases or greased bun tins. Bake for 15–20 minutes at 375°F., Gas mark 5.

Rock cakes

8 oz. self-raising flour
pinch salt
1 teaspoonful mixed spice
3 oz. butter or margarine
3 oz. caster sugar
3 oz. mixed dried fruit
1 egg
2–3 teaspoonfuls milk (enough to make a stiff
    mixture)

Prepare mixture by the rubbing-in method, see page 19. Place teaspoonfuls of the mixture on greased baking trays in rocky heaps. Bake for 10–15 minutes at 400°F., Gas mark 6.

Raspberry buns

8 oz. self-raising flour
pinch salt
3 oz. butter or margarine
3 oz. caster sugar
1 egg
2–3 teaspoonfuls milk (enough to make a stiff dough)
raspberry jam

Prepare mixture by the rubbing-in method, see page 19, divide into 12 pieces and shape each lightly into a ball. Place on greased baking trays. Make a little hole in each bun and fill it with jam. Bake for 10–15 minutes at 400°F., Gas mark 6.

Coffee cream buns

8 oz. self-raising flour
pinch salt
3 oz. butter or margarine
3 oz. caster sugar
1 egg
2 teaspoonfuls instant coffee
2–3 teaspoonfuls milk (enough to make a stiff dough)

Prepare mixture by the rubbing-in method, see page 19, adding the coffee dissolved in the milk. Place teaspoonfuls of the mixture on greased baking trays in rocky heaps. Bake for 10–15 minutes at 400°F., Gas mark 6. When cool, split each bun through the centre and fill with coffee butter cream, using 3 oz. butter etc., see page 50.

Ginger cakes

5 oz. self-raising flour
pinch salt
1 teaspoonful ground ginger
$\frac{1}{4}$ teaspoonful ground cinnamon
3 oz. butter or margarine
2 oz. soft brown sugar
1 oz. almonds, chopped
4 teaspoonfuls black treacle
4 teaspoonfuls golden syrup
1 egg
2 tablespoonfuls milk

Prepare mixture by the rubbing-in method, see page 19. Divide the mixture between 18–20 paper baking cases or greased bun tins. Bake for 15–20 minutes at 375°F., Gas mark 5.

Orange sandwich

Coconut sandwich

Add 1 oz. desiccated coconut and 1 tablespoonful milk. When cold, cut in 2 and sandwich with jam, dust with sieved icing sugar.

Walnut sandwich

Add 2 oz. walnuts, coarsely chopped. When cold, cut in 2 and sandwich with coffee butter cream, see page 50.

Chocolate sandwich

4 oz. butter or margarine
4 oz. caster sugar
3½ oz. self-raising flour
½ oz. drinking chocolate
2 teaspoonfuls cocoa
pinch salt
2 eggs
2 oz. plain chocolate, melted in 1 tablespoonful milk
few drops vanilla essence
apricot jam

Grease an 8-inch sandwich tin and line with grease-proof paper. Prepare mixture by the creaming method, see page 19, place mixture into the prepared tin and smooth level. Bake for 30—35 minutes at 375°F., Gas mark 5. When cool, split in 2 and sandwich with apricot jam. Top with chocolate fudge icing, using half-quantity, recipe on page 51.

Victoria sandwich

2 eggs, their weight (in shells) in butter or
  margarine, self-raising flour and caster sugar
pinch salt
3—4 drops vanilla essence

Grease 1 x 8-inch or 2 x 7-inch sandwich tins and line the base(s) with a round of greaseproof paper. Prepare mixture by the creaming or one-stage method, see pages 19 and 20, place into the prepared tin(s) and smooth level. Bake the 7-inch tins for 20—25 minutes, the 8-inch tin for 30 minutes—both at 375°F., Gas mark 5. When cold, cut in 2, spread with jam, sandwich together and dust the top with sieved icing sugar.

Variations

Orange sandwich

Omit vanilla essence, add grated rind ½ orange and 2 teaspoonfuls orange juice. When cold, cut in 2 and sandwich together and top with orange honey cream using 3 oz. icing sugar etc., see page 51. If liked decorate with orange marzipan fruits.

Madeira cake

4 oz. butter or margarine
5 oz. caster sugar
8 oz. self-raising flour
pinch salt
2 eggs
2 tablespoonfuls milk
few drops vanilla essence or a little lemon rind,
  grated
thin strip citron peel (optional)

Grease and line a 6-inch round cake tin. Prepare mixture by the creaming or one-stage method, see pages 19 and 20. Place mixture into the tin, smooth level and lay the strip of citron peel on top. Bake for 1 hour at 350°F., Gas mark 4.

Fruit cake

4 oz. butter or margarine
4 oz. caster sugar
8 oz. self-raising flour
$\frac{1}{4}$ teaspoonful salt
2 eggs
2$\frac{1}{2}$ fl. oz. milk
grated rind 1 lemon or 1 orange
9 oz. mixed dried fruit

Grease and line a 6-inch round cake tin. Prepare mixture by the creaming or one-stage method, see pages 19 and 20. Place mixture into the tin and smooth level. Bake for 1$\frac{1}{2}$ hours at 350°F., Gas mark 4.

Cut and come again cake

8 oz. self-raising flour
$\frac{1}{4}$ teaspoonful salt
2 teaspoonfuls mixed spice
4 oz. butter or margarine
4 oz. caster sugar
9 oz. mixed dried fruit
1 teaspoonful grated orange or lemon rind
1 egg + enough milk and water mixed to make up
  to $\frac{1}{4}$ pint

Grease and line a 6-inch round cake tin. Prepare mixture by the rubbing-in method, see page 19. Place mixture into the tin and smooth level. Bake for approximately 1$\frac{1}{4}$ hours at 350°F., Gas mark 4.

Simnel cake

6 oz. butter or margarine
6 oz. soft brown sugar
9 oz. self-raising flour
pinch salt
$\frac{1}{2}$ teaspoonful mixed spice
3 eggs
$\frac{1}{8}$ pint milk
2 teaspoonfuls golden syrup
1 lb. currants
2 oz. raisins
4 oz. sultanas
1 oz. glacé cherries, chopped
4 oz. cut mixed peel
almond paste using **6 oz.** ground almonds etc., see
  page 52

To finish:
almond paste using **6 oz.** ground almonds etc.
1 tablespoonful apricot jam
little beaten egg

Grease and line an 8-inch cake tin. Make up the almond paste as directed. Prepare cake mixture by the creaming method, see page 19. Put half of the mixture into the tin, smooth level. Roll out the almond paste to fit the tin and place on top of the cake mixture. Put the remaining cake mixture on top and smooth level. Bake in the centre of the oven for 1 hour at 350°F., Gas mark 4 then reduce the temperature to 275°F., Gas mark 1 and bake for a further 2$\frac{1}{2}$ hours. The cake should be allowed to mature for at least two weeks before finishing.

Roll out half of the almond paste to an 8-inch round on sugared greaseproof paper. Heat the jam in a small saucepan until boiling, brush over the top of the cake. Place the round of almond paste on top, press down firmly and trim the edges to neaten. Make the remaining almond paste into 12 small balls and arrange in a ring round the outer edge of the cake, attaching them with a little beaten egg. Brush the balls with beaten egg. Tie a piece of greaseproof paper round the outside of the cake. Place the cake into a moderate oven 350°F., Gas mark 4 for 10–15 minutes to brown the top.

If liked, when the cake is cool, finish with a little glacé icing, see page 51, in the centre and add a few sugar Easter eggs for decoration.

Date and walnut cake

4 oz. butter or margarine
4 oz. caster sugar
12 oz. self-raising flour
$\frac{1}{4}$ teaspoonful salt
$\frac{1}{2}$ teaspoonful mixed spice
2 eggs
$\frac{1}{4}$ pint milk and water mixed
2 tablespoonfuls warmed golden syrup
6 oz. dates, stoned and chopped
1$\frac{1}{2}$ oz. walnuts, chopped

Grease and line an 8-inch round cake tin. Prepare mixture by the creaming or one-stage method, see pages 19 or 20. Place mixture into the tin and smooth level. Bake for 1$\frac{1}{4}$ hours at 350°F., Gas mark 4.

Chocolate cake

5 oz. butter or margarine
5 oz. caster sugar
8 oz. self-raising flour
pinch salt
3 eggs
1 tablespoonful milk
5 oz. plain chocolate, melted in a basin over hot
water

Grease and line a 7-inch cake tin. Prepare mixture by the creaming method, see page 19. Place mixture into the tin and smooth level. Bake for 1 hour 10 minutes at 350°F., Gas mark 4.

Cherry cake

6 oz. glacé cherries
4 oz. butter or margarine
4 oz. caster sugar
7 oz. self-raising flour
pinch salt
3 eggs
1 oz. ground almonds

Grease and line a 6-inch round cake tin. Quarter the cherries and toss in a little of the weighed flour. Prepare mixture by the creaming method, see page 19. Place mixture into the tin and smooth level. Bake for 1¼ hours at 350°F., Gas mark 4.

Cherry almond cake

4–6 oz. cherries
8 oz. butter or margarine
8 oz. caster sugar
8 oz. plain flour
pinch salt
3 eggs
few drops almond essence
4 oz. ground almonds

Grease and line an 8-inch round or 7-inch square cake tin. Quarter the cherries and toss in a little of the weighed flour. Prepare mixture by the creaming method, see page 19, the fat and sugar must be creamed very thoroughly.
Place mixture into the tin and smooth level. Bake for about 3¼ hours at 275°F., Gas mark 1.

🥄 Note the use of plain flour for this cake. When making cherry cakes it is very important to remove the syrup from the glacé cherries so that they will be evenly distributed in the cake. This can be done by tossing the quartered cherries in a little flour or by washing the syrup off—if this is done the cherries must be dried thoroughly before using.

Coffee walnut cake

6 oz. butter or margarine
6 oz. caster sugar
8 oz. self-raising flour
pinch salt
3 eggs
1 tablespoonful instant coffee dissolved in 1
tablespoonful milk
2–4 oz. walnuts, chopped

Grease and line a 7-inch round or 6-inch square cake tin. Prepare mixture by the creaming method, see page 19. Place the mixture into the tin and smooth level. Bake for 1 hour 10 minutes at 350°F., Gas mark 4.

Dundee cake

6 oz. butter or margarine
6 oz. granulated or soft brown sugar
4 oz. self-raising flour
4 oz. plain flour
¼ teaspoonful salt
1 teaspoonful mixed spice
3 eggs
1 tablespoonful milk
15 oz. mixed dried fruit
2 oz. split almonds for decoration

Grease and line a 7-inch round cake tin. Prepare mixture by the creaming method, see page 19, place in tin and smooth level; arrange split almonds on top in an attractive pattern. Bake for 1 hour at 350°F., Gas mark 4, reduce heat to 300°F., Gas mark 2 and bake for a further 1¼ hours.

Christmas cake 1

6 oz. butter or margarine
6 oz. brown or granulated sugar
10 oz. self-raising flour
pinch salt
1 teaspoonful mixed spice
3 eggs
2 tablespoonfuls milk
1 tablespoonful black treacle, warmed
1 tablespoonful brandy (optional)
1¼ lb. mixed dried fruit
grated rind 1 orange

Grease and line an 8-inch round or 7-inch square cake tin. Prepare mixture by the creaming method, see page 19, place in tin and smooth level. Bake for 1 hour at 350°F., Gas mark 4, reduce heat to 275°F., Gas mark 1 and bake for a further 2 hours.

This makes a slightly lighter cake than Christmas cake 2.

Christmas cake 2

8 oz. butter or margarine
8 oz. soft brown sugar
½ teaspoonful gravy browning
8 oz. plain flour
pinch salt
½ teaspoonful ground nutmeg
1 teaspoonful mixed spice
4 eggs
3 tablespoonfuls brandy
8 oz. currants
8 oz. raisins
8 oz. sultanas
2 oz. glacé cherries, chopped
2 oz. cut mixed peel
2 oz. blanched almonds, chopped

Grease and line an 8-inch round or 7-inch square tin. Prepare mixture by the creaming method, see page 19, place in tin and hollow out the centre slightly. Bake for 4½ hours at 275°F., Gas mark 1.

Rich dark cake

8 oz. butter or margarine
6 oz. soft brown or granulated sugar
12 oz. self-raising flour
¼ teaspoonful salt
½ teaspoonful ground nutmeg
6 tablespoonfuls milk
1 tablespoonful black treacle, warmed
3 eggs
1 tablespoonful gravy browning
1¾ lb. mixed dried fruit
grated rind 1 orange (optional)

Grease and line an 8-inch round or 7-inch square cake tin. Prepare mixture by the creaming method, see page 19, place in tin and smooth level. Bake for 1 hour at 350°F., Gas mark 4, reduce heat and bake a further 2 hours at 275°F., Gas mark 1.

Gingerbread

12 oz. self-raising flour
pinch salt
4 teaspoonfuls ground ginger
2 teaspoonfuls ground cinnamon
6 oz. butter or margarine
8 oz. black treacle
6 oz. soft brown sugar
2 eggs
¼ pint milk

Grease and line a 7-inch square cake tin. Prepare mixture by the melting method, see page 19, pour into the tin. Bake for 1½ hours at 325°F., Gas mark 3.

Parkin

4 oz. self-raising flour
4 teaspoonfuls ground ginger
8 oz. medium oatmeal
2 oz. butter or margarine
8 oz. black treacle
4 oz. soft brown sugar
1 egg
2–3 tablespoonfuls milk

Grease a Yorkshire pudding tin approximately 9 by 7 inches. Prepare mixture by the melting method, see page 19, pour into the prepared tin and spread evenly. Bake for 1 hour at 325°F., Gas mark 3, shelf below middle.

Sponge cake

2 eggs
3 oz. caster sugar
3 oz. self-raising flour
pinch salt

Prepare a greased 8-inch sandwich tin by mixing together 1 teaspoonful flour and 1 teaspoonful caster sugar and dusting the tin with the flour and sugar mixture. This gives a characteristic sugary finish to the sponge. Prepare mixture by the whisking method, see page 19, spread evenly into the prepared tin. Bake for 20 minutes at 350°F., Gas mark 4.

Christmas cake

Swiss roll

2 eggs
2½ oz. caster sugar
2 oz. self-raising flour
pinch salt

To finish:
jam, warmed
caster sugar

Grease and line a 9 by 13 inch Swiss roll tin. Prepare mixture by the whisking method, see page 19, spread evenly into the tin. Bake for 10 minutes at 425°F., Gas mark 7, third shelf from top. Turn out sponge upside down on to a sheet of greaseproof paper dusted with caster sugar. Peel off the lining paper and trim off the edges of the sponge with a sharp knife. Spread the warmed jam thinly over the sponge and roll up at once.

Chocolate log

3 oz. butter or margarine
3 oz. caster sugar
3 oz. self-raising flour
pinch salt
2 teaspoonfuls cocoa
1 oz. drinking chocolate
2 eggs

To finish:
apricot jam
chocolate butter cream using 8 oz. icing sugar etc.,
    see page 50

Make and bake as for Swiss roll, spreading with apricot jam before rolling up. When cold, completely cover the Swiss roll with chocolate butter cream. Mark with a fork to resemble the bark of a tree, dust lightly with icing sugar.

Genoese sponge

3 eggs
4 oz. caster sugar
3 oz. self-raising flour
pinch salt
3 oz. butter or margarine, melted and cooled

Grease and line a Swiss roll tin approximately 7 by 10 inches. Prepare mixture by the whisking method, see page 19, adding the cooled fat after the flour has been folded in. Spread mixture evenly into the tin. Bake for 25 minutes at 375°F., Gas mark 5. When cold cut into fancy shapes or fingers; ice and decorate.

Cake fillings and icings

Butter cream

To sandwich and top a 7-inch sandwich cake or sandwich an 8-inch sandwich cake:

2 oz. butter
4 oz. icing sugar, sieved
2 teaspoonfuls hot milk
flavouring (see below)

Beat the butter until soft, gradually beat in icing sugar, milk and any flavouring.

Flavourings for butter cream

Vanilla
Add a few drops of vanilla essence.

Chocolate
Add 1 oz. plain chocolate, grated, and melted with the 2 teaspoonfuls hot milk.

Orange
Add finely grated rind ½ orange and a few drops orange colouring.

Peppermint
Add a few drops peppermint essence and a few drops green colouring.

Coffee
Add 1 teaspoonful instant coffee dissolved in the milk.

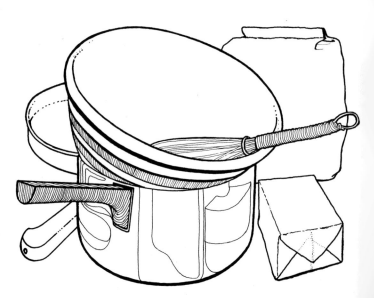

Lemon curd cream

2 oz. butter
3 oz. icing sugar, sieved
2 tablespoonfuls lemon curd

Beat butter until soft, gradually beat in icing sugar and lemon curd.

Orange honey cream

2 oz. butter
3 oz. icing sugar, sieved
1 tablespoonful thick honey
finely grated rind ½ orange

Beat butter until soft, gradually beat in icing sugar, honey and orange rind.

Glacé icing

8 oz. icing sugar, sieved
about 2 tablespoonfuls water
squeeze lemon juice

Place sugar in small saucepan, add water and lemon juice. Add colouring, if liked, heat gently for 1 minute then use at once.

Flavourings for glacé icing

Coffee
Add 2 tablespoonfuls instant coffee.

Chocolate
Sieve 1 tablespoonful cocoa with the icing sugar.

Orange
Use strained orange juice or orange squash in place of the water.

Fudge icing

to sandwich or top an 8-inch cake:
1 small can condensed milk
4 oz. sugar
3 oz. butter or margarine
few drops vanilla essence

Place all the ingredients into a thick-bottomed saucepan, heat gently until the sugar dissolves. Simmer gently stirring frequently until a little of the mixture forms a soft ball when dropped into cold water (about 5 minutes). Beat well until thick and use as desired.

Chocolate fudge icing

2 oz. butter or margarine
3 tablespoonfuls milk
few drops vanilla essence
2 tablespoonfuls cocoa
8 oz. icing sugar, sieved

Melt butter and milk, stir in the vanilla essence and cocoa. Mix well and gradually beat in the icing sugar. Cool until thick, beating well from time to time.

Rich chocolate icing

4 oz. plain chocolate
½ **oz.** butter
2 tablespoonfuls water
6 oz. icing sugar, sieved

Melt chocolate, butter and water over a gentle heat. Beat in the icing sugar.

Whipped cream
Use double or whipping cream, place in a chilled bowl and beat with a fork or rotary whisk until soft peaks are formed. Care should be taken at this stage because over-whipping will make the cream separate. Spreading or piping the cream also thickens it further, and should be done lightly.

Covering rich fruit cakes with almond paste and royal icing

Make the cake at least 6—8 weeks before it is required and store it in clean greaseproof paper and foil in a cool dry place. The surface to be iced should be as flat and even in shape as possible. Smooth over slight irregularities with the almond paste.

If you wish to keep a cake for some time after icing, allow the almond paste to dry out for a week or so before the Royal icing is put on. This minimises the risk of almond oil discolouring the white icing. If you plan to cover the cake with 1 coat of Royal icing, do this the day before the cake is decorated and allow to dry overnight. For 2 coats of icing allow 2 days.

Time for decorating depends on the design: allow 1—3 days for this. If you are using 2 coats of Royal icing and the design is so intricate that it will take 3 days to complete, apply the almond paste 2 weeks before the cake is required. For a simpler cake, say, with 1 coat of icing and a maximum of 1 day's decoration, apply the almond paste 11 days before the cake is required. If you haven't time to allow the paste to dry out completely, brush it with egg white and leave for 24 hours before applying icing.

Almond paste

12 oz. sugar (usually **6 oz.** caster and **6 oz.** icing
    sugar)
12 oz. ground almonds
1 egg or 3 egg yolks
juice $\frac{1}{2}$ lemon, strained
flavouring to taste (for example, $\frac{1}{2}$ teaspoonful vanilla
    essence and $\frac{1}{2}$ teaspoonful almond essence)

Sieve the sugars into bowl, add ground almonds and
mix well. Beat up egg in a basin, add lemon juice and
flavourings. Pour egg mixture on to dry ingredients
and mix to a pliable paste using a fork. If the paste is
sticky, work in a little more sugar, if too stiff, work in a
little lemon juice.

Avoid handling the paste more than absolutely necessary or the warmth of your hands will draw
the oil out of the almonds, making the paste very
difficult to roll out.

Applying almond paste

Dust a sheet of greaseproof paper with caster sugar.
Knead the paste very lightly and cut off just under
half of it. Roll this smaller piece on the sugared paper
into a round a little larger than the diameter of the
cake. Brush one side of the paste with beaten egg or
sieved apricot jam boiled until thick, place cake on it
(if necessary, add a little paste to make the cake
surface level or, if the cake base is more even than the
top side, apply paste to the base). Press firmly, trim off
surplus paste and neaten edges, using a knife.

Using a piece of string, measure the circumference of
the cake and mark this on a fresh sheet of sugared
paper (see above). Roll out remaining paste into a
long strip a little wider than the depth of the cake.
Trim and neaten ends and one long edge of the strip,
brush with egg or jam. Turn the cake on its side, lift
carefully on to the paste so the straight edge is level
with the paste-covered top of the cake. Place one
hand behind the paper and roll cake along the strip
of paste until the sides are covered. Trim off surplus
paste. Turn over cake carefully so the almond-pasted
top is resting on the paper. Trim off extra from base
of sides and neaten join, using table knife. Roll a
straight-sided jar or tin around the sides so the paste
sticks firmly to the cake. If necessary hold a ruler
vertically against the sides of the cake to make sure
it is level—this is particularly important for a tiered
cake. Turn the cake over carefully, roll the jar or tin
once round the sides. Cover the cake lightly with
fresh greaseproof paper, stand it on an upturned
plate and place in a cool dry place for 3—7 days.

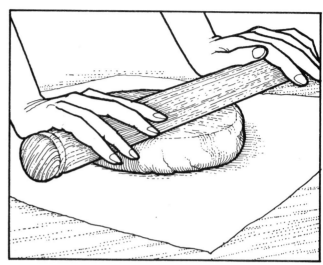

*Rolling out the almond paste on a sheet of greaseproof
paper dusted with caster sugar.*

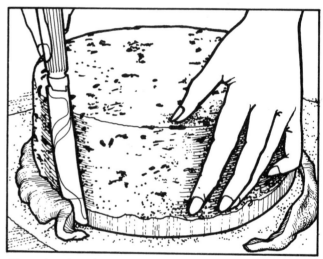

*The cake placed on the round of almond paste and the
surplus paste being trimmed off with a knife.*

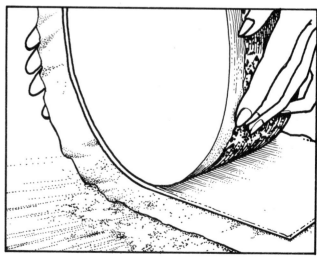

*The side of the cake placed on the strip of almond paste
and being rolled along the strip until the sides are covered.*

The cake upside-down and the surplus almond paste being trimmed from the bottom.

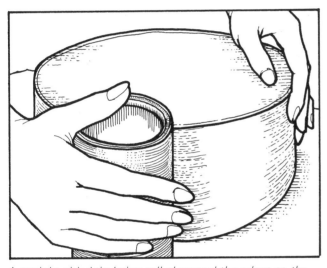

A straight-sided tin being rolled around the edges so the paste will stick firmly to the cake.

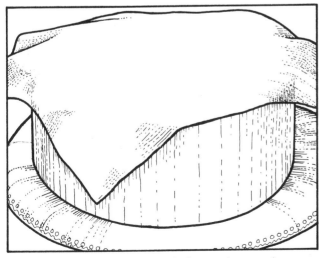

The cake placed on an upturned plate and covered lightly with clean greaseproof paper.

When applying almond paste to the sides of a large round cake, divide larger portion of paste into 2, roll each portion into a long thin strip a little longer than **half** the circumference of the cake and proceed as before, neatening the extra join. For a square cake divide remaining portion of the paste into 4 and cover sides 1 at a time, joining the corners neatly.

How much almond paste to use

Size of cake	Area covered	Quantity required
round 6 inch or 5 inch square	top only	3 oz. ground almonds etc.
round 6 inch or 5 inch square	top and sides	6 oz. ground almonds etc.
round 7 inch or 6 inch square	top only	4 oz. ground almonds etc.
round 7 inch or 6 inch square	top and sides	8 oz. ground almonds etc.
round 8 inch or 7 inch square	top only	5 oz. ground almonds etc.
round 8 inch or 7 inch square	top and sides	10 oz. ground almonds etc.
round 9 inch or 8 inch square	top only	6 oz. ground almonds etc.
round 9 inch or 8 inch square	top and sides	12 oz. ground almonds etc.
round 10 inch or 9 inch square	top only	8 oz. ground almonds etc.
round 10 inch or 9 inch square	top and sides	16 oz. ground almonds etc.
round 11 inch or 10 inch square	top only	10 oz. ground almonds etc.
round 11 inch or 10 inch square	top and sides	20 oz. ground almonds etc.
round 12 inch or 11 inch square	top only	12 oz. ground almonds etc.
round 12 inch or 11 inch square	top and sides	24 oz. ground almonds etc.

Icing the cake

There are three items which make icing a cake easier: a metal ruler for smoothing the top, a plastic bowl scraper for the sides and a revolving icing table. All 3 are well worth investing in if you ice your own cakes. Choose a cake board 2 inches larger than the cake, put a thin layer of icing in the centre of the board and press the cake down on to it. Leave about 20–30 minutes for the icing to harden. Spread the icing smoothly on the top of the cake, using a round bladed knife and working it on in a circular movement to get rid of any air bubbles. Dip the metal ruler in boiling water, shake to get rid of surplus moisture. Hold it firmly at each end and draw it quickly and evenly over the top at an angle of 45 degrees.

Repeat if necessary until the surface of the cake is flat and smooth. Remove surplus icing from the sides of the cake and if possible allow the top to dry before icing the sides. Place the cake on a revolving icing table and spread icing evenly over the sides. When a square cake is being iced, it is best to cover the sides one at a time, removing surplus icing from the corners with a sharp knife. Dip a plastic bowl scraper in cold water and shake off the surplus moisture. Hold it against the side of the cake with the finger spread out to exert even pressure and revolve the table. Finish off with a quick movement towards you. Repeat if necessary until the sides are smooth.

Hold a knife against the top edge of the cake and shave off the icing to make a groove for piping. Allow to dry and if necessary apply a second coat. Leave the surplus icing in a small bowl covered with a damp cloth, ready for decorating the cake.

Decorating the cake

It is a good plan to draw the design on a piece of greaseproof paper first, before starting on the cake. If this is done to scale, it can be placed on the top of the cake and marked through with a clean pin to give a guide for piping.

To make a paper icing bag

Use greaseproof paper or vegetable parchment. Cut a square of paper about 10 by 10 inches and divide into 2 triangles (the size of the square can vary according to the amount of piping to be done but avoid too large a bag, as it is difficult to hold and manipulate for fine work). Take one triangle and fold A over to C as shown. Wrap B round to A and C and fold in the ends. Cut about ½ inch off the point and insert the pipe. Repeat with the other triangle. Greaseproof paper icing bags can only be used once but vegetable parchment can be wiped clean and re-used. Ready-made nylon icing bags or metal or plastic syringes can also be used.

Filling the bag

Insert the pipe, half-fill the bag with icing, using a teaspoon. Fold over the broad end and tuck in the sides (if the bag is too full the icing will squeeze out of the sides).

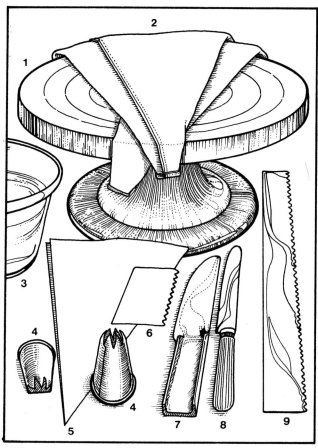

1 icing table; 2 icing bags; 3 bowl of water; 4 icing nozzles; 5 greaseproof paper; 6 and 7 plastic scrapers; 8 round bladed knife; 9 metal ruler.

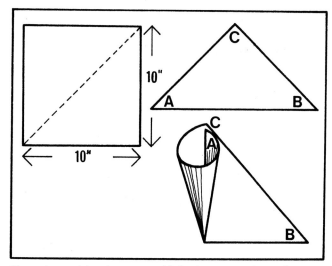

To make an icing bag cut a 10-inch square piece of greaseproof paper and divide into two. Fold A to C.

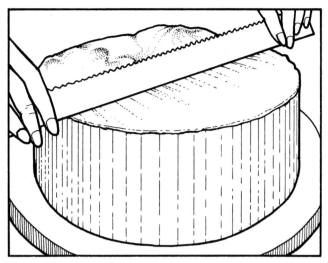

Smoothing the surface by drawing a metal ruler quickly and evenly over the top at an angle of 45 degrees.

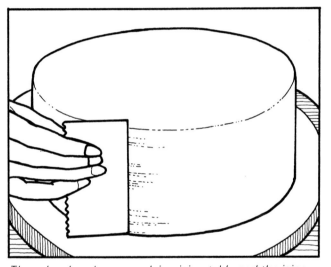

The cake placed on a revolving icing table and the icing being spread evenly over the sides.

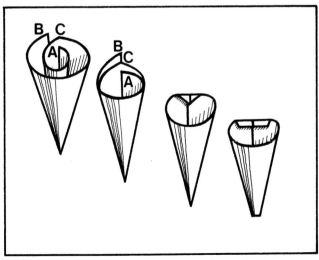

Wrap B round to A and C and fold in the ends. Cut about ½ inch off the point.

Royal icing

approximately 1½ lb. icing sugar
2–3 drops lemon juice or 1½ teaspoonfuls glycerine
4 egg whites

Sieve icing sugar through a fine sieve. Break up egg whites in a mixing bowl using a fork, but do not beat. Add icing sugar gradually, beating well between each addition until the icing is a fairly thick cream. Add lemon juice or glycerine. Continue beating until the icing is white, smooth, feels 'velvety' and is the consistency of thick cream. Vigorous beating is essential. If the icing is left to stand in between beatings, or at any time during use, cover it with a damp cloth to prevent a 'crust' forming on top. If you are using an electric mixer: place egg whites in bowl, beat lightly with a fork. Add icing sugar gradually on speed 1 or 2, then beat at speed 2 or 3 for 5–8 minutes. Allow icing to stand 1½–2 hours or overnight before use, covered with a well damped cloth to release the air bubbles.

Lemon juice hardens the icing, glycerine prevents it from becoming unduly hard if the cake is to be kept for any length of time.

How much royal icing for 1 coat and simple decoration

6 inch round cake or 5 inch square	12 oz. icing sugar, 2 egg whites etc.
7 inch round cake or 6 inch square	about 1¼ lb. icing sugar, 3 egg whites etc.
8 inch round cake or 7 inch square	1¼–1½ lb. icing sugar, 3–4 egg whites etc.
9 inch round cake or 8 inch square	1½ lb. icing sugar, 4 egg whites etc.
10 inch round cake or 9 inch square	1¾–2 lb. icing sugar, 5 egg whites etc.
11 inch round cake or 10 inch square	2¼ lb. icing sugar, 6 egg whites etc.
12 inch round cake or 11 inch square	2½–2¾ lb. icing sugar, 7 egg whites etc.

d icings

Scones, teabreads and biscuits

Plain scones

8 oz. self-raising flour
pinch salt
2 oz. butter or margarine
1 oz. caster sugar
$\frac{1}{4}$ pint milk

Mix flour and salt, rub in fat. Stir in sugar and add milk. Mix to a soft dough and turn on to a floured board. Knead lightly and roll out to just under $\frac{1}{2}$ inch thick. Cut into rounds and place on a greased baking tray. Knead the trimmings together lightly and cut out 1 or 2 more rounds. Bake for 10–12 minutes at 425°F., Gas mark 7, second shelf from top.

Fruit scones

Add 2 oz. currants or sultanas with the milk. Make up and bake as for Plain scones.

Date and walnut scones

8 oz. self-raising flour
pinch salt
2 oz. butter or margarine
1 oz. soft brown sugar
2 oz. dates, finely chopped
1 oz. walnuts, chopped
$\frac{1}{4}$ pint milk

Make up and bake as for Plain scones, see above.

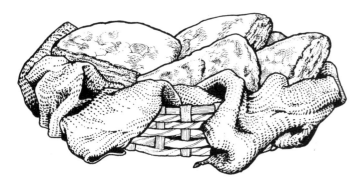

Girdle scones

8 oz. self-raising flour
pinch salt
1 oz. butter or margarine
1 tablespoonful sugar
$\frac{1}{4}$ pint + 2 tablespoonfuls milk

Mix the flour and salt, rub in the fat. Stir in the sugar and add the milk. Mix to a soft dough and turn on to a floured board. Divide the dough in two and knead very lightly. Roll out to a 6- or 7-inch round and cut into 6. Cook on a greased girdle over a low heat, turning when well risen, and golden brown on the underside. Cool the scones between the folds of a clean tea-towel placed on a cooling tray.

Cheese scones

8 oz. self-raising flour
$\frac{1}{4}$ teaspoonful salt
$\frac{1}{2}$ teaspoonful dry mustard
pinch pepper
1$\frac{1}{2}$ oz. butter or margarine
3 oz. cheese, finely grated
$\frac{1}{4}$ pint milk

Sieve together flour, salt, mustard and pepper. Rub in fat and stir in cheese. Add milk and proceed as for Plain scones, see opposite.

Savoury scones

8 oz. self-raising flour
pinch salt
pinch pepper
1$\frac{1}{2}$ oz. butter or margarine
1 oz. cheese, finely grated
2 oz. bacon, grilled until crisp
$\frac{1}{4}$ pint milk

Sieve together flour, salt and pepper. Rub in fat, stir in cheese and bacon which has been finely crumbled. Add milk and proceed as for Plain scones, see opposite.

Potato scones

1 oz. butter or margarine
3 oz. self-raising flour
12 oz. cooked mashed potato
salt; pepper

Rub fat into flour, mix with the cold mashed potato and a little salt and pepper. Turn on to a floured board and knead until smooth. Divide into 3 pieces and roll each to a round about 6 inches in diameter, cut into 4. Cook for 2–3 minutes on each side on a fairly hot, greased girdle until golden brown. Serve hot and buttered or when cold fry in hot bacon fat and serve for breakfast.

Plain scones; fruit scones; potato scones; treacle scones, page 58; dropped scones, page 58

56

Treacle scones

8 oz. self-raising flour
pinch salt
1½ oz. butter or margarine
1 oz. soft brown sugar
2 tablespoonfuls black treacle (about **2 oz.**)
just under ¼ pint milk

Mix flour and salt, rub in fat and stir in sugar. Warm milk slightly and blend in treacle. Add to the rubbed-in mixture and proceed as for Plain scones, see page 56.
If liked the scone mixture can be shaped into a round, marked into four, and baked on a greased baking tray.

Dropped scones

4 oz. self-raising flour
pinch salt
1½ oz. caster sugar
1 large egg
milk to mix (about 4–5 tablespoonfuls)

Mix flour, salt and sugar. Add the egg and gradually beat in the milk to make a smooth fairly thick batter. Drop dessertspoonfuls of the mixture on to a greased, moderately hot girdle. Cook until the tops of the scones are covered with bubbles and the undersides are golden brown. Turn and brown on the other side (about 3–4 minutes in all). Cool the scones between the folds of a clean tea-towel placed on a cooling tray.

Welsh cakes

8 oz. self-raising flour
½ teaspoonful salt
4 oz. butter or margarine
2 oz. caster sugar
2 oz. currants
1 egg
2 tablespoonfuls milk

Mix flour and salt, rub in fat. Add sugar and currants and mix to a fairly stiff dough with the egg and milk. Knead lightly and roll out to ¼ inch thick. Cut into 2-inch rounds and cook on a moderately hot greased girdle for 2–3 minutes on each side. Cool the scones on a cooling tray.

Skye shortbread

Shortbread:
8 oz. plain flour
pinch salt
2 oz. caster sugar
4 oz. butter or margarine

Topping:
4 tablespoonfuls apricot jam
1 egg white
3 oz. icing sugar, sieved
2 oz. almonds, chopped

Grease an 11 by 7 inch Swiss roll tin. Mix flour, salt and caster sugar, rub in the fat thoroughly. Spread the mixture into the tin and press down firmly. Spread the jam over the shortbread mixture. Beat the egg white until frothy and add the icing sugar. Mix well and spread over the jam; sprinkle with almonds. Bake for 1 hour 20 minutes at 300°F., Gas mark 2 and cut into fingers while warm.

Butter fingers

Shortbread:
8 oz. plain flour
pinch salt
2 oz. caster sugar
4 oz. butter or margarine

Topping:
2 oz. butter
2 oz. demerara sugar

Grease an 11 by 7 inch Swiss roll tin. Prepare the shortbread mixture as in recipe for Skye shortbread. Bake for 25 minutes at 325°F., Gas mark 3.
Meanwhile soften the butter, add the demerara sugar and beat well. Spread the topping evenly over the hot shortbread and return to the oven for 5 minutes. Cut into fingers while still warm.

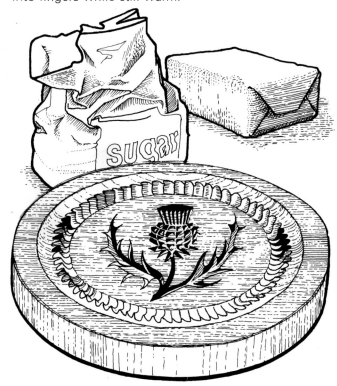

Grantham gingerbreads

4 oz. margarine
4 oz. caster sugar
1 tablespoonful beaten egg
4 oz. self-raising flour
4 teaspoonfuls ground ginger

Cream margarine and sugar. Stir in the egg and the flour sieved with the ground ginger. Roll into small balls and place on greased baking trays; bake for 45 minutes at 275°F., Gas mark 1, shelf below middle.

Gingerbread men

10 oz. self-raising flour
pinch salt
3 teaspoonfuls ground ginger
2 oz. margarine or butter
3 tablespoonfuls golden syrup
4 oz. caster sugar

Decoration:
currants
glacé cherries

Prepare mixture by the melting method, see page 19. Leave until cool enough to handle. Grease firm baking trays, shape portions of mixture into gingerbread men shapes and place on the trays. Mark 'eyes' with currants and put some down the 'body' as buttons.

Gingerbread men

Use a piece of curved glacé cherry for the mouth. Bake for 15–20 minutes at 325°F., Gas mark 3. Ease each 'man' from the baking trays while still warm.

Melting moments

5 oz. self-raising flour
pinch salt
1½ oz. margarine
2½ oz. cooking fat
3 oz. caster sugar
½ an egg
quick cooking oats
glacé cherries

Mix the flour and salt. Cream the margarine and cooking fat, add the sugar and cream again. Beat in the egg and a little flour. Stir in the rest of the flour and salt. Divide the mixture in 12–14 pieces. Roll each into a ball and toss in oats. Place on greased baking trays without flattening. Decorate each melting moment with a piece of glacé cherry and bake in a moderate oven, 350°F., Gas mark 4, for 15 minutes.

Variation:
For chocolate melting moments, use 4 oz. self-raising flour and 1 oz. cocoa, sieved together, then proceed as above.

59

Hungarian chocolate biscuits

Hungarian chocolate biscuits

4 oz. butter or margarine
2 oz. caster sugar
4 oz. self-raising flour
1 oz. cocoa
½ teaspoonful vanilla essence

Filling:
chocolate butter cream using **2 oz.** butter etc., see
page 50

Prepare mixture by the creaming method, see page
19. Roll mixture into balls the size of a small marble
and place on a greased baking tray. Flatten the balls
with a fork dipped in cold water and bake for 10
minutes at 375°F., Gas mark 5. When the biscuits
are quite cold, sandwich together with the butter
cream and dredge with sieved icing sugar.

Empire biscuits

5 oz. butter or margarine
3 oz. caster sugar
8 oz. self-raising flour
pinch salt
1 egg yolk

To finish:
3 tablespoonfuls jam
glacé icing using **8 oz.** icing sugar etc., coloured
and flavoured to taste, see page 51

Prepare mixture by the creaming method, see page
19. Leave paste in a cool place for about 1 hour before
cutting out the biscuits. Roll out mixture to about
⅛ inch in thickness and cut out with a 2–2½-inch
cutter. Place biscuits on greased baking trays and
bake for 15–20 minutes at 325°F., Gas mark 3. When
the biscuits are cold, sandwich them together with
jam and ice with glacé icing.

Almond jumbles

2 oz. butter or margarine
2 oz. caster sugar
3 oz. self-raising flour
pinch salt
1 tablespoonful beaten egg
2 oz. ground almonds
few drops almond essence

To decorate:
glacé cherries or chopped almonds

Prepare mixture by the creaming method, see page 19.
Pipe out in rosettes through a forcing bag on to a
greased baking tray or alternatively place teaspoon-

fuls of the mixture on to the baking tray. Put a tiny piece of glacé cherry or sprinkle chopped almonds on the top and bake for 20 minutes at 325°F., Gas mark 3.

Florentines

4 oz. caster sugar
4 oz. margarine
4 tablespoonfuls golden syrup
3 oz. glacé cherries
2 oz. blanched almonds
1½ oz. hazelnuts or walnuts
4 oz. self-raising flour
pinch salt
1 teaspoonful vanilla essence

Coating:
8 oz. plain chocolate

Warm the sugar, fat and syrup in a large saucepan, avoiding overheating. Cut cherries into 6 or 8 depending on the size, chop nuts coarsely. Mix flour and salt, add to warmed ingredients with vanilla essence, nuts and cherries, beat thoroughly and allow to cool. Grease a firm baking tray and put the mixture on it in teaspoonfuls about 3 inches apart. Bake in a moderate oven, 350°F., Gas mark 4, for 10–12 minutes until deep golden brown. When the biscuits have been in the oven for 5 minutes, remove the baking tray from the oven and, using a plain scone cutter, pull the edges of each biscuit together. Return to the oven to finish cooking. Allow to cool a little before removing from the tin with a knife. Leave to cool on a wire tray; refill the baking tray and proceed as before.
To finish the biscuits: cut the chocolate into small pieces, place in a bowl and melt over hot water or in the oven. Avoid overheating or the chocolate will lose its gloss. Using a knife, spread the back of the Florentines with chocolate and draw a clean comb through the chocolate to ridge it. When the chocolate is set, store the biscuits in an airtight tin.

Gipsy creams

3 oz. butter or margarine
3 oz. caster sugar
4 oz. self-raising flour
pinch salt
4 teaspoonfuls cocoa
2 tablespoonfuls hot water
2 teaspoonfuls syrup, warmed
2½ oz. rolled oats

Filling:
2 oz. butter or margarine
1 tablespoonful syrup
2 tablespoonfuls cocoa

Prepare mixture by the creaming method, see page 19. Put small teaspoonfuls of the mixture on to greased baking trays and bake for 20 minutes at 350°F., Gas mark 4.
To make the filling: cream the butter and syrup and gradually sieve in the cocoa. When the biscuits are quite cold, sandwich them together with a little of the filling.

Grasmere shortcake

8 oz. self-raising flour
pinch salt
½ teaspoonful ground ginger
4 oz. soft brown sugar
4 oz. butter or margarine

Filling:
2 oz. butter or margarine
4 oz. icing sugar
1 teaspoonful syrup from the ginger
3–4 pieces stem ginger

Grease and line an 11 by 7 inch Swiss roll tin. Sieve flour, salt, ginger and brown sugar into a mixing bowl and rub in the fat. Press the mixture into the tin, spreading it evenly. Bake for 25 minutes at 325°F., Gas mark 3. Turn the cake out when cooked and trim the edges. Cut into 2 pieces while still hot, then allow to cool before adding the filling.
To make the filling: beat the fat until soft, add the sieved icing sugar and the syrup and beat thoroughly. Fold in the chopped ginger. Spread evenly on one half of the cake, place the other half on top. Cut into fingers.

Garibaldi biscuits

4 oz. self-raising flour
pinch salt
1 oz. butter or margarine
1 oz. caster sugar
1–2 tablespoonfuls milk

Filling:
2 oz. currants or other dried fruit

Prepare mixture by the rubbing-in method, see page 19. Turn the dough on to a floured board, knead lightly into shape and roll out to ⅛ inch thick. Roll evenly, keeping the dough regular in shape, then cut into 2. Sprinkle one half evenly with the fruit. Cover with the other half and roll the mixture again until ⅛ inch thick, keeping it as square as possible. Trim the edges, then mark into squares or fingers. Place on a greased baking tray and bake for 15–20 minutes at 350°F., Gas mark 4. Lift on to a cake rack, then separate the biscuits.

Rich chocolate biscuits

1½ **oz.** plain chocolate
1 tablespoonful milk
4 oz. self-raising flour
pinch salt
1 oz. caster sugar
2½ **oz.** margarine
few drops vanilla essence

Filling:
chocolate butter cream using **2 oz.** butter etc., see
 page 50

Shred the chocolate with a knife, put in a small basin
or teacup with the milk and dissolve over hot water.
Mix together flour and salt, and rub in margarine.
Stir in the sugar, add the essence and melted chocolate. Bind to a paste and leave until firm enough to
handle. Roll out paste to ⅛ inch thick and cut into
rounds using a 2-inch fancy cutter. Place on greased
baking trays, prick well with a fork and bake for 20
minutes at 325°F., Gas mark 3. When cold, sandwich
the biscuits together with the butter cream and dust
the tops with sieved icing sugar.

Easter biscuits

3 oz. margarine
3 oz. caster sugar
8 oz. self-raising flour
good pinch salt
½ teaspoonful mixed spice
about ½ a beaten egg for mixing
3 oz. currants

Prepare the mixture by the creaming method, see
page 19, adding only sufficient egg to make a stiff
dough. Roll out the dough on a floured board until
about ⅛ inch in thickness. Cut into rounds with a
cutter 3 inches in diameter. Place the biscuits on
greased baking trays and bake in a very moderate
oven, 325°F., Gas mark 3 for 20 minutes.

Chocolate chip cookies

4 oz. butter or margarine
2 oz. caster sugar
6 oz. self-raising flour
2 tablespoonfuls condensed milk
4 oz. plain chocolate, chopped

Prepare the mixture by the creaming method, see
page 19. Take teaspoonfuls of the mixture and roll
into balls. Place on greased baking trays and flatten
with a fork.
Bake in a moderate oven, 350°F., Gas mark 4 for
about 15 minutes.

Date and walnut loaf

Malt loaf

12 oz. self-raising flour
pinch salt
2 oz. caster sugar
4 oz. sultanas
4 tablespoonfuls malt extract
2 oz. butter or margarine
2 eggs
¼ pint milk

Grease a 2-lb. loaf tin and line the base with greaseproof paper. Mix the flour, salt, sugar and sultanas.
Warm the malt and fat until the fat melts. Add to the
dry ingredients, gradually mixing in the eggs and
milk to make a soft dough. Pour into the prepared tin,
bake for 1 hour 10 minutes at 325°F., Gas mark 3.

Date and walnut loaf

12 oz. self-raising flour
pinch salt
2 oz. caster sugar
4 oz. dates, chopped
2 oz. walnuts, broken up
2 oz. butter or margarine
4 tablespoonfuls golden syrup
2 eggs
¼ pint milk

Prepare as for Malt loaf, see opposite, melting the golden syrup with the fat.
Bake for 1 hour 10 minutes at 325°F., Gas mark 3.

Jamaican ginger loaf

12 oz. self-raising flour
pinch salt
1 teaspoonful ground ginger
2 oz. caster sugar
3 oz. sultanas
1 oz. stem ginger, chopped
2 oz. butter or margarine
4 tablespoonfuls warmed black treacle
2 eggs
$\frac{1}{4}$ pint milk

Prepare as for Malt loaf, see opposite, melting the treacle with the fat.
Bake for 1 hour 10 minutes at 325°F., Gas mark 3.

Orange sultana loaf

12 oz. self-raising flour
pinch salt
2 oz. caster sugar
4 oz. sultanas
4 tablespoonfuls orange marmalade
2 oz. butter or margarine
2 eggs
$\frac{1}{4}$ pint milk

Prepare as for Malt loaf, see opposite, melting the marmalade with the fat.
Bake for 1 hour 10 minutes at 325°F., Gas mark 3.

Bun loaf

12 oz. self-raising flour
$\frac{1}{4}$ teaspoonful salt
1 teaspoonful mixed spice
4 oz. butter or margarine
4 oz. caster sugar
4 oz. currants
2 oz. sultanas
2 oz. raisins
1 oz. mixed peel
$\frac{1}{2}$ **oz.** walnuts, chopped
1 egg
$\frac{1}{4}$ pint milk
3 tablespoonfuls marmalade

Grease a 2-lb. loaf tin and line the base with grease-proof paper. Prepare mixture by the rubbing-in method, see page 19. Put into the prepared tin and smooth level. Bake for 2 hours at 300°F., Gas mark 2, shelf below middle.

Brack

8 oz. sultanas
4 oz. stoned raisins
4 oz. currants
6 oz. demerara sugar
$\frac{1}{4}$ pint tea, strained
8 oz. self-raising flour
1 egg

Put sultanas, raisins and currants into a basin with the sugar. Pour over the tea and leave overnight.
The following day, stir in the flour and the well beaten egg. Bake for 1$\frac{1}{2}$ hours at 325°F., Gas mark 3, in a greased and lined loaf tin 9 by 5 inches. Keep for a few days before cutting.

Cinnamon crunch loaf

8 oz. self-raising flour
pinch salt
3 oz. margarine
3 oz. caster sugar
1 egg beaten with $\frac{1}{4}$ pint milk
4 tablespoonfuls strawberry jam

Topping:
1 oz. self-raising flour
2 oz. caster sugar
1 teaspoonful cinnamon
1$\frac{1}{2}$ oz. margarine

Grease a 9 by 5 inch loaf tin, line the base with greaseproof paper. Mix together the flour and salt. Rub in the margarine and stir in the sugar. Add the egg and milk and beat until smooth. Place half of the dough into the tin and smooth level. Spread over the jam and top with the remaining dough.
To make the topping, mix the dry ingredients and rub in the margarine. Sprinkle the crumble over the dough and bake for 1 hour at 350°F., Gas mark 4.

Yeast cookery

Fresh yeast can usually be obtained from a good baker provided you order it a day or two in advance. In place of fresh yeast, the dried variety can be bought at most large food stores and grocers. Remember when substituting dried for fresh yeast that $\frac{1}{2}$ **oz.** dried yeast = **1 oz.** fresh yeast.
To reconstitute dried yeast, take $\frac{1}{4}$ pint of the measured liquid, heat until tepid and pour into a small jug or bowl. Stir in 1 teaspoonful sugar and sprinkle the yeast on to the liquid. Cover and leave in a warm place until frothy—about 10–15 minutes. Fresh yeast should be creamed with a little of the measured liquid before use. It may be stored in a polythene bag for 4–5 days in a cold place, up to 4 weeks in a refrigerator and up to 6 months in a home freezer.

White bread

3 lb. strong plain flour
1 oz. salt
1 oz. lard or cooking fat (optional)
1 oz. fresh yeast or $\frac{1}{2}$ **oz.** dried yeast + 1
 teaspoonful sugar
approximately $1\frac{1}{2}$ pints water

1. Sieve flour and salt, rub in fat, if used.
2. Prepare yeast liquid (see above).
3. Add yeast liquid and remaining liquid to flour mixture.
4. Mix well then turn on to a board and knead thoroughly for 10 minutes.
5. Place dough into greased bowl and place bowl inside a large greased polythene bag.
6. Leave until dough has doubled in size.

This can be done in a cold or warm place, cold rising gives best results but warm rising is quicker. The approximate times for rising are as follows: 1 hour in a warm place; 2 hours at room temperature; 12 hours at a low temperature; 24 hours in the refrigerator.

7. Turn dough on to a lightly floured board and knead well for about 5 minutes.
8. Grease 4 x 1-lb. or 2 x 2-lb. loaf tins.
9. Cut dough into 2 or 4 pieces and shape neatly to fit the tins.
10. Place inside a large greased polythene bag and leave until the dough rises to the tops of the tins— the time will again depend on the temperature.
11. Preheat the oven to 475°F., Gas mark 9, reduce heat to 400°F., Gas mark 6 and bake 1-lb. loaves for 40 minutes, 2-lb. loaves for 1 hour. If you like crustier loaves, turn the loaves on to a baking tray after baking and return to the oven for 5 minutes.

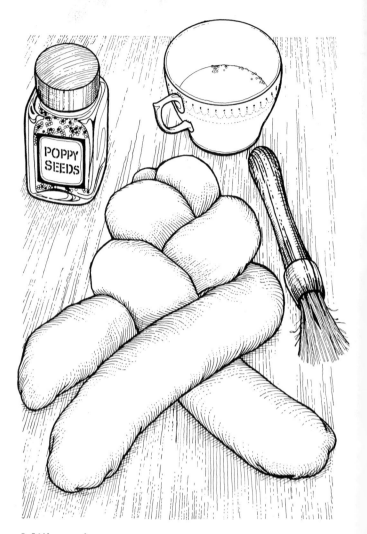

Milk twist

1 lb. strong plain flour
2 teaspoonfuls salt
$\frac{1}{2}$ **oz.** lard or cooking fat
$\frac{1}{2}$ **oz.** fresh yeast or 1 teaspoonful dried yeast + 1
 teaspoonful sugar
$\frac{1}{4}$ pint milk
$\frac{1}{4}$ pint water

To finish:
beaten egg
poppy seeds (optional)

Follow steps 1–7 of White bread recipe, see opposite. Divide dough into 3 and roll each piece into a long sausage. Plait the 3 pieces together, brushing the ends with beaten egg to secure firmly. Place on a greased baking tray and place inside a large greased polythene bag. Leave until dough has doubled in size, brush with beaten egg and sprinkle with poppy seeds. Bake for 30–35 minutes at 400°F., Gas mark 6.

Milk twist; simple currant bread, page 66; Aberdeen butteries, page 66; hot cross buns, page 67; Chelsea buns, page 67

Bread rolls

half-quantity White bread recipe, using 1½ lb. strong plain flour etc., see page 64

Glaze:
1 egg
large pinch salt

To decorate:
poppy seeds (optional)

Follow steps 1–7 of recipe for White bread, see page 64. Divide dough into about 18 2-oz. pieces; shape into rolls. Place on greased baking trays and place inside greased polythene bags to rise. When doubled in size brush with the egg beaten together with salt and sprinkle with poppy seeds. Bake for 20 minutes at 425°F., Gas mark 7, second shelf.

Simple currant bread

1 lb. strong plain flour
2 teaspoonfuls salt
1 oz. butter or margarine
4 oz. currants
1 oz. caster sugar
1 oz. fresh yeast or ½ **oz.** dried yeast + 1
   teaspoonful sugar
¼ pint milk
¼ pint water

Glaze:
honey or golden syrup

Follow steps 1–4 of White bread recipe, see page 64, adding the currants and sugar after the fat has been rubbed in. Halve dough and shape each piece to fit a greased 1-lb. loaf tin. Place tins inside a large greased polythene bag and leave until dough has doubled in size. Bake for 30 minutes at 400°F., Gas mark 6. While hot, brush the tops with a wet pastry brush dipped in honey or golden syrup.

Aberdeen butteries

1 lb. strong plain flour
2 teaspoonfuls salt
1 oz. sugar
1 oz. fresh yeast or ½ **oz.** dried yeast + 1
   teaspoonful sugar
½ pint water
5 oz. lard
5 oz. butter or margarine

Follow directions for White bread recipe steps 1–7, see page 64, adding the sugar to the dry ingredients.

Beat together lard and butter and chill. After the second kneading, roll out to a strip about 14 inches long. Place a third of the fat in small pieces over the top two thirds of the dough. Fold up the bottom third, then fold down the top third. Give a half-turn to the right. Repeat the rolling and folding twice more with the remaining fat. Roll out just under ½ inch thick and cut into about 10 pieces—the shape is not important. Place on ungreased baking trays. Place the baking trays inside large, greased polythene bags and leave until dough has doubled in size. Bake for 20 minutes at 400°F., Gas mark 6.

Lardy cake

half quantity of White bread recipe, using 1½ lb. strong plain flour etc., see page 64

6 oz. lard
8 oz. soft brown sugar

Follow steps 1–7 as for White bread recipe, see page 64. Roll out dough to a strip 10 by 18 inches. Place a third of the lard over the dough in small pieces, sprinkle with a third of the sugar. Fold up the bottom third and fold down the top third. Repeat the rolling and folding with another portion of lard and sugar and roll out to approximately 8 inches square. Place in a greased roasting tin and place tin inside a large greased polythene bag. When dough has doubled in size, score the top lightly. Melt the remaining lard and brush a little over the dough. Bake for 20 minutes at 400°F., Gas mark 6, pour over the remaining lard and sprinkle with the remaining sugar. Bake for a further 20 minutes.

Pizza

Yeast dough:
8 oz. strong plain flour
¼ teaspoonful salt
1 oz. butter or margarine
½ **oz.** fresh yeast or 1 teaspoonful dried yeast +
   1 teaspoonful sugar
¼ pint milk

Topping:
1 small onion, peeled and chopped
1 tablespoonful oil
1 x 8-oz. can tomatoes
1 tablespoonful tomato purée
½ teaspoonful mixed herbs
salt; pepper
sugar
6 oz. cheese, thinly sliced
1 small can anchovy fillets, drained
black olives

Prepare dough as for White bread, steps 1–7, see page 64. Meanwhile, gently fry the onion in oil until soft but not brown. Stir in the tomatoes, tomato purée and herbs, cook for about 10 minutes or until thick. Season to taste, cool. Roll out dough to a 9-inch round. Place on a greased baking tray and spread with the tomato mixture. Cover with the cheese and arrange the anchovy fillets in a lattice pattern on top. Decorate with olives and leave in a warm place for 15 minutes. Bake for 25–30 minutes at 425°F., Gas mark 7.

Rum babas

4½ oz. plain flour
pinch salt
3¾ fl. oz. milk
¼ oz. fresh yeast or **½** teaspoonful dried yeast + 1 teaspoonful sugar
2 eggs
1¾ oz. butter or margarine, softened
½ oz. caster sugar

Rum syrup:
3 oz. granulated sugar
7½ fl. oz. water
3 tablespoonfuls rum
squeeze lemon juice
whipped cream, optional

Mix flour and salt; prepare the yeast liquid. Add the eggs and yeast liquid to flour, beat well; place bowl inside a large polythene bag and leave in warm place for about 1 hour. Beat in the butter and caster sugar. Divide the mixture between 8–10 greased individual ring tins. Leave until mixture rises almost to the tops of the tins. Bake for 10–15 minutes at 400°F., Gas mark 6.
Make the syrup while the babas are cooking: dissolve the sugar in the water. Simmer for 5 minutes, add rum and lemon juice. Turn out the babas and spoon the syrup over. Serve hot, or allow to cool and pipe whipped cream in centre of each baba.

Hot cross buns

½ oz. fresh yeast or 1 teaspoonful dried yeast + 1 teaspoonful sugar
½ pint milk
1 lb. plain flour
1 teaspoonful salt
1 teaspoonful mixed spice
2 oz. caster sugar
2 oz. butter or margarine
3 oz. currants
1 oz. cut mixed peel
1 egg, beaten

To make crosses:
2 oz. plain or self-raising flour
water to mix

Glaze:
2 tablespoonfuls milk
2 tablespoonfuls water
2 tablespoonfuls sugar

Prepare the yeast liquid then make up the mixture by the rubbing-in method, see page 19. Place the dough into a greased bowl and place the bowl inside a large, greased polythene bag. Leave until dough has doubled in size then knead well and divide into 2-oz. pieces. Shape the buns and place on greased baking trays; place the trays inside large greased polythene bags and leave until buns have doubled in size.
Meanwhile, to make the 'crosses', mix flour to a soft dough with water. Place inside a greaseproof paper piping bag, see page 54. When the buns have risen, snip the end off the piping bag and pipe a 'cross' on each bun. Bake for 10 minutes at 425°F., Gas mark 7. While the buns are baking, heat together the ingredients for the glaze until the sugar dissolves and simmer for 2 minutes. Brush over the buns and bake them for a further 5 minutes.

Chelsea buns

Yeast dough:
½ oz. fresh yeast or 1 teaspoonful dried yeast + 1 teaspoonful sugar
¼ pint + 2 tablespoonfuls milk
1 lb. plain flour
½ teaspoonful salt
2 oz. caster sugar
2 oz. butter or margarine
2 eggs, beaten

Filling:
1 oz. butter or margarine
2 oz. caster sugar
1 teaspoonful mixed spice
4 oz. currants

Prepare yeast liquid, then make up dough by the rubbing-in method, see page 19. Place dough into a greased bowl and place the bowl inside a large, greased polythene bag, leave until dough has doubled in size. Knead well and roll out to a square 18 by 18 inches. Melt the fat and brush over the dough. Sprinkle with the sugar and spice, mixed together, then the currants. Roll up lightly and cut into 16 pieces. Arrange cut-side down in a greased roasting tin or 2 greased cake tins. Place the tin(s) in large greased polythene bags and leave until buns have doubled in size. Bake for 30 minutes at 375°F., Gas mark 5. While hot brush with a sugar glaze (see glaze for Hot cross buns, above).

Cooking for special occasions

You can, of course, leave the whole business to caterers—hire everything from plates to premises while you sit back with your feet up. The chances are, though, that even if mounting costs and multiplying guest lists don't put a stop to it, you yourself will want more than a hand in the festivities . . . All you need is a large refrigerator (and that can easily be hired if yours isn't large enough), a few hardworking friends and a lot of forethought. If you also have a freezer, so much the better.

If this is your first attempt at catering on a large scale, start by getting yourself a large notebook and making lists of absolutely everything you'll need, from guests, invitation cards, flowers, flower vases, food, furniture (or removal of it), plates, glasses, cups—everything down to the last cream bun. Leave nothing to chance, however unforgettable it may seem. Then enlist help, fix a date—and make a start.

Do as much as possible in advance—our notes will help you with this (look for the small spoon sign)— and, if it's to be a big occasion, leave as many of the last-minute tasks to someone else as possible: even hire help if necessary. All the good food and perfect catering in the world won't make your special occasion a success if you, the hostess, are hot, harassed, and mostly in the kitchen . . .

Wedding receptions

Hold them at home, at a friend's or relative's house, or, if something larger is needed, hire a small hall (the church hall, perhaps) or clubroom in which you can do the catering yourself. Such rooms may not have full catering facilities, but they will certainly have the wherewithal to make tea and coffee and probably equipment for keeping food warm. Whatever their facilities, if they are pleasing the rooms will certainly be in great demand throughout the year, so as soon as a date has been decided, make hiring the premises your first task—you may even have to fix the date round the premises. Remember that if you are having a church wedding the church must also be 'booked', and you will probably find this equally difficult, particularly in spring and early summer.
Once these two major hurdles have been overcome, however, you can start working methodically through your list, checking off first all 'durable' items, such as cutlery, glasses, tables, tablecloths and so on, before moving on to the perishables—flowers, food, drink— not forgetting the cake and a good sharp knife to cut it with. If you are holding the reception at home, see that the room is ready the night before and any surplus furniture removed. Lay out all cold food before the wedding service and cover it with plastic film or foil.

Champagne may be served throughout the reception though tea or coffee is usually served whilst the bride and bridegroom are changing. Alternatively offer a drink (sherry for example) or a selection of drinks when the guests arrive and reserve champagne for the toasts and the cake.

Food at weddings usually falls into one of two categories: cocktail-type snacks or a more substantial buffet meal. The former is obviously easiest and the following suggestions will provide ample refreshment (recipes where applicable on pages 69–70):

Cheese straws	
Anchovies on toast	allow 2 per head
Cheese and olive biscuits	allow 2 per head
Salted almonds	allow 8 oz. for 25
Vol-au-vents	allow 2 per head
Pizza tartlets	allow 2 per head
Cocktail sausages on sticks	allow 2–3 per head
Potato crisps	1 large packet for 25
Stuffed olives	9-oz. jar for 25

Buffet meals require more time and planning, but if you limit the choice to a selection of the following savouries and sweets you will find it quite within your scope, and your efforts will certainly be appreciated (recipes on page 70–77):

Savouries
Cream cheese horns
Filled bridge rolls
Asparagus or smoked salmon rolls
Sausage rolls, see page 29
Deep-fried scampi or goujons of plaice with tartare sauce
Cold 'kebabs'
Meat balls with chutney sauce
Prawn mayonnaise tartlets
Curried chicken tartlets
Sausage pinwheels, see page 90

Paella with celery and lettuce salad, see page 109
Assorted savoury flans, see page 29
Liver and gherkin triangles
Cold salmon cutlets
Salmon and cucumber mousse, see page 112
Assorted cold meats and poultry, thinly sliced
Chicken liver pâté
Mixed fish pâté
Chicken and pork pâté
Waldorf salad
Tossed green salad, see page 112
Selection of cheeses with crispbread, rolls and butter

Sweets
Fruit salad
Sherry trifle
Apricot crown gâteau
Brandied coffee charlotte
Cream caramels
Frangipane flan
Strawberries and cream
Plain and coffee meringues, see page 84
Chocolate éclairs, see page 37
Pineapple nut slice

Cocktail snacks

Cheese straws

cheese pastry using 4 oz. flour, see page 16

Roll out the pastry $\frac{1}{4}$ inch thick. Cut out strips 3 inches long and $\frac{1}{4}$ inch wide. Transfer carefully to greased baking trays. Re-roll trimmings and cut out rings using 2 cutters—one slightly larger than the other. Bake for 10–15 minutes or until golden brown at 325°F., Gas mark 3, shelf just above the middle. Serve bundles of straws through the rings and decorate with sprigs of parsley.

Anchovies on toast
Place drained anchovy fillets or halved sardines on fingers of cold buttered toast. Decorate with gherkin slices.

Cheese and olive biscuits
Spread cream cheese or cottage cheese on small biscuits and decorate with slices of stuffed olives or tomato.

Salted almonds
Gently fry whole blanched almonds in a mixture of butter and oil, turning once, until golden brown. Drain on absorbent paper and toss in salt whilst hot. A selection of salts, for example onion, garlic and celery can be used.

Vol-au-vents
These can be bought, either large or small. Fill them cold with: chopped hardboiled eggs with mustard and cress in mayonnaise; flaked tuna fish or salmon in white sauce or mayonnaise; cooked vegetables in white or cheese sauce; diced chicken with chutney; diced lamb with red currant jelly; diced beef with horseradish sauce.
Or fill them hot with: creamed mushrooms (canned); diced chicken in white or cheese sauce; mixed cooked vegetables in sauce; flaked smoked fish in parsley, white or cheese sauce; diced meat in curry sauce.

Pizza tartlets

makes 20:
shortcrust pastry using 6 oz. flour etc., see page 16

1 onion, peeled and chopped
1 oz. butter or margarine
½ **oz.** plain flour
1 x 8-oz. can tomatoes
4 tablespoonfuls water
½ teaspoonful mixed dried herbs
salt; pepper
2 oz. cheese, grated

Roll out pastry thinly and line 20 tartlet tins. Fry onion in melted fat until soft, with the lid on the pan. Stir in flour and cook for 1 minute. Add tomatoes with their juice, water, herbs and seasonings. Bring to the boil, stirring all the time. Cover and simmer for 5 minutes. Cool slightly and pour into the pastry cases, sprinkle with the cheese and bake for 20 minutes at 375°F., Gas mark 5, middle shelf and shelf above the middle. Serve hot or cold.

Opposite: Fruit salad, page 73 or page 103
Above: Deep-fried goujons of plaice with tartare sauce

Buffet dishes

Cream cheese horns

Make cream horns as directed on page 35, brushing with beaten egg before baking. Fill with a mixture of cream or cottage cheese and diced cucumber.

Filled bridge rolls

Split in half, butter and cover with any of the fillings suggested on page 82.

Asparagus or smoked salmon rolls

Remove crusts from thin slices of buttered brown bread. Roll up round an asparagus tip or thin slice of smoked salmon. Wrap in damp greaseproof paper until required.

As a variation, use thin frankfurter sausages with mustard.

Deep-fried scampi or goujons of plaice with tartare sauce

Coat scampi or thin strips (goujons) of plaice with beaten egg and breadcrumbs. Deep fry in hot fat or oil until golden.

Quick tartare sauce

Use sandwich spread or add chopped capers and gherkins to mayonnaise or salad cream.

Cold 'kebabs'

Arrange cooked cocktail sausages, gherkins, small pickled onions, tomato wedges and tiny bacon rolls on cocktail sticks and serve stuck into a grapefruit or small melon.

Meat balls with chutney sauce

makes 40:
1 lb. raw minced beef
1 x 3½-oz. packet sage and onion stuffing mix
salt; pepper
1 egg, beaten

Mix together meat and dry stuffing mix, season with salt and pepper and bind with the beaten egg. Shape into 40 small balls. Fry in shallow fat or oil for about 5–10 minutes until crisp and golden. Serve hot or cold on cocktail sticks accompanied with chutney sauce.

As a variation, try Pork balls: mix 1 lb. pork sausage meat with ½ packet sage and onion stuffing mix, made up according to the instructions on the packet. Season with a little mustard, salt and pepper. Shape and fry as above.

Prawn mayonnaise tartlets

makes 24:
shortcrust pastry using 8 oz. flour etc., see page 16

Filling:
2 x 7-oz. cans prawns, drained
¼ pint mayonnaise, see page 25
chopped parsley

Line 24 tartlet tins with the pastry. Prick well and bake for 10–12 minutes or until golden brown at 400°F., Gas mark 6.
Allow to cool. Reserve a few prawns for decoration. Pile remainder into the cases. Coat with mayonnaise, using a teaspoon. Decorate with remaining prawns and parsley.

Curried chicken tartlets

24 tartlet cases made and baked as for Prawn mayonnaise tartlets, see above

Filling:
1 small onion, finely chopped
1 tablespoonful oil
1 tablespoonful curry powder
1 tablespoonful mango chutney
¼ pint stock
3 tablespoonfuls mayonnaise,
   see page 25
4 oz. cooked chicken, diced

Fry the onion in the heated oil until soft; add curry powder. Cook 1 minute then stir in chutney and stock. Simmer until thick, allow to cool. Add curry mixture to mayonnaise, season to taste. Stir in the chicken and fill the pastry cases.

Liver and gherkin triangles

makes 8:
flaky pastry using 8 oz. plain flour etc.,
see page 16

Filling:
8 oz. liver sausage, diced
8 gherkins, chopped

Roll out the pastry thinly and cut into 8 squares. Mix together the liver sausage and gherkin and place a little in the centre of each pastry square. Brush pastry edges with beaten egg, fold over to form triangles. Press edges well together and crimp. Place on a wetted baking tray, brush with beaten egg and bake for 10–15 minutes at 425°F., Gas mark 7, shelf just above the middle.
Serve hot or cold.

Mixed fish pâté

Cold salmon cutlets

Allow 1 x 8-oz. cutlet for 2 people: wrap each cutlet in buttered foil, sprinkled with a little lemon juice, pepper and salt. Bake for about 20 minutes at 325°F., Gas mark 3. Unwrap the foil and test fish against the bone to check that it is cooked before removing from the oven. Allow to cool slightly, then remove the skin and bone. Divide each steak in 2 lengthways. When cold, coat with mayonnaise, see page 25. Decorate with cucumber and sprigs of parsley. Serve on a platter decorated with a ring of shredded lettuce.

Chicken liver pâté

serves 6:
1 medium onion, peeled and chopped
1 clove garlic, peeled and crushed
1 bay leaf
4 oz. butter
8 oz. chicken livers, washed and dried
salt; freshly milled black pepper
2 tablespoonfuls brandy

Fry onion, garlic and bay leaf in 2 oz. of the butter until soft. Add chicken livers and fry for about 4–5 minutes (the liver should still be pink inside). Sieve or liquidise, beat in remaining 2 oz. softened butter, seasoning and brandy. Pour into a small loaf tin or individual pots, cover with a layer of clarified butter. Chill. Serve cold with toast fingers.

The pâté may be made 2 days beforehand and stored, covered, in the refrigerator.

To clarify butter, heat gently until frothy, strain.

Mixed fish pâté

serves 8:
1 x 7-oz. can salmon, drained and flaked, with skin and bones removed
1 x 7-oz. can tuna fish, drained and flaked
1 x 7-oz. can prawns, chopped
5 tablespoonfuls single cream
4 oz. butter, softened
grated rind and juice 1 lemon
salt; freshly milled black pepper

Beat all ingredients together until smooth. Press into a pudding basin and chill. Turn out and decorate with fresh prawns and parsley. Serve with toast fingers.

The pâté may be made the day before and stored, covered, in the refrigerator.

Chicken and pork pâté

serves 12–14:
8 oz. pig's liver, minced or finely chopped
8 oz. lean pork, minced
8 oz. sausagemeat
1 onion, peeled and finely chopped
1 tablespoonful chopped parsley
2 oz. soft white breadcrumbs
2 tablespoonfuls brandy
a little beaten egg
$\frac{1}{4}$ teaspoonful nutmeg
salt; black pepper
8 rashers streaky bacon, de-rinded
2 chicken breasts, skinned and flattened
1 bay leaf

Mix together liver, pork, sausagemeat, onion, parsley, breadcrumbs, brandy, egg and seasoning. Stretch bacon rashers with the back of a knife and use four to line the base of a greased 2-lb. loaf tin. Spread over half the stuffing mixture, cover with flattened chicken breasts. Cover with remaining stuffing and place remaining bacon on top with the bay leaf.
Cover loaf tin with foil and place tin in a roasting tin half-filled with hot water. Cook in centre of oven for 1½–2 hours at 350°F., Gas mark 4. Remove loaf tin from roasting tin and weight the top of the pâté. Allow to cool completely.

Waldorf salad

serves 10:
1 head celery, washed and chopped
1 lb. red apples, cored and chopped
3–4 oz. walnuts, roughly chopped
grated rind and juice 1 lemon
mayonnaise using $\frac{1}{2}$ pint oil, see page 25

Mix together celery, apples, walnuts and lemon rind and toss in the lemon juice. Combine salad with enough mayonnaise to give a smooth coating. Serve chilled.

This salad is best eaten the same day.

Fruit salad

serves 25–30:
1 x 14-oz. can strawberries
1 x 10-oz. can fruit salad
1 x 16-oz. can pears
1 x 10-oz. can black cherries
1 x 16-oz. can apricot halves
1 x 16-oz. can sliced peaches
4 oz. sugar
$\frac{1}{2}$ pint water
3 bananas, peeled and sliced
3 apples, washed, cored and diced
3 oranges, peeled and divided into segments
juice 1 lemon
1–2 pints single cream to serve

Dice the canned fruits. Mix together with the syrup from the cans. Dissolve the sugar in the water and boil for 2 minutes. Add the lemon juice and pour mixture on to the canned fruit. Leave overnight in a cold place. Add the fresh fruit on the day the fruit salad is required and serve with cream.

Sherry trifle

serves 25:
20 individual sponge cakes
raspberry or strawberry jam
30 macaroons
48 ratafia biscuits
grated rind 2 oranges
1 pint sherry
2½ pints custard

To decorate:
1 pint double cream
½ pint single cream
glacé cherries
angelica leaves
5 oz. flaked almonds

Split sponge cakes and sandwich together with jam.
Cut up roughly and divide between 4 glass dishes.
Sprinkle over the crumbled macaroons, ratafias and
orange rind. Pour over the sherry and allow to soak
for 2–3 hours before covering with custard. Brown
the almonds under a moderate grill, cool and store
in a polythene bag.
To decorate the trifle, whip the creams until soft
peaks form. Spread a layer of cream over each trifle:
decorate with cherries, angelica leaves and browned
almonds.

The basic trifle may be made 2 days in advance: decorate on the day of serving.

Apricot crown gâteau

serves 8:
3 x 7-inch Victoria sandwiches: one and a half times
the recipe using 3 eggs etc., see page 45

Filling and decoration:
1 x 15½-oz. can apricot halves, drained, reserving
  juice
4 tablespoonfuls apricot jam
½ pint double cream, whipped
24 sponge finger biscuits
a little apricot glaze

To decorate:
orange ribbon

Spoon a little of the apricot juice over the cakes
and sandwich together with apricot jam and some of
the whipped cream. Spread remaining cream around
the sides of the cake and press on sponge finger
biscuits. Arrange apricots on top of cake and brush
with apricot glaze. Tie ribbon around the middle of
the cake. Decorate top and bottom edge of cake
with remaining piped cream. Serve chilled.

The Victoria sandwiches may be made 2
days in advance and decorated on the day required.

Brandied coffee charlotte

serves 10:
6 oz. unsalted butter
6 oz. caster sugar
1 tablespoonful coffee powder dissolved in
  1 tablespoonful hot water
6 oz. ground almonds
2 tablespoonfuls brandy
½ pint double cream, whipped
24 sponge finger biscuits or coffee meringue
  fingers, trimmed to size

Cream together butter and sugar until light and
fluffy. Beat in the coffee essence, almonds and
brandy. Fold in two-thirds of the whipped cream.
Transfer mixture to a 6-inch deep round cake tin
lined on the base with greaseproof paper. Chill
overnight in refrigerator. Turn out, press sponge
finger biscuits around the sides of the charlotte and
decorate top with remaining cream. Serve chilled.
If liked decorate with coffee bean sweets.

Brandied coffee charlotte

Sherry trifle, page 74

Cream caramels

makes 12:
Caramel:
6 oz. granulated sugar
6 tablespoonfuls water

Custard:
9 large eggs, beaten
6 oz. caster sugar
1½ teaspoonfuls vanilla essence
2¼ pints milk

Dissolve granulated sugar in water, stirring occasionally. Boil until a good caramel colour is obtained, pour into 12 heated ¼-pint pudding tins. Beat together eggs, sugar and vanilla essence. Heat the milk (do not boil) and pour on to eggs. Strain custard mixture into tins, place in roasting tins half-filled with hot water (be careful the water does not come over the sides of the pudding tins) and cook just below centre of oven at 350°F., Gas mark 4 for 45 minutes or until custard is set. Remove, allow to become completely cold before turning out. Serve chilled, decorated with piped cream.

These may be made up to 4 days before and kept in the refrigerator.

Frangipane flan

serves 8:
flan pastry using 6 oz. flour etc., see page 16

Filling:
3 tablespoonfuls apricot jam
2 oz. butter or margarine
2 oz. caster sugar
1 egg, beaten
½ teaspoonful almond essence
½ teaspoonful vanilla essence
½ oz. plain flour
2 oz. ground almonds

Topping:
a few whole blanched almonds
glacé icing using **3 oz.** icing sugar etc., see page 51

Roll out pastry fairly thinly and use to line an 8-inch fluted flan ring. Lightly prick the base with a fork and spread with apricot jam. Prepare filling by the creaming method, see page 19, spread over jam to edges of flan. Roll out pastry trimmings and cut into strips. Arrange in a criss-cross pattern on top of almond mixture. Place whole almonds in spaces of criss-cross design. Bake at 375°F., Gas mark 5, in centre of oven for 30 minutes or until golden. Spread glacé icing over flan while still hot. Allow to cool

Pineapple nut slice

before removing from flan case. Serve cold with single cream.

🥄 This may be made 1 day in advance.

Pineapple nut slice

serves 8:
1 slab sponge cake (use Swiss roll, see page 50)
1 x 7½-oz. can pineapple rings, drained, reserving juice
3 tablespoonfuls sherry
½ pint double cream, whipped
2 oz. flaked almonds, browned
apricot glaze, see page 105
a few cocktail cherries, halved

Cut sponge cake into 3 equal-sized oblongs. Mix 4 tablespoonfuls pineapple juice with sherry and spoon over the sponge cakes. Sandwich cakes together with some of the whipped cream. Spread remaining cream around sides of the cake and press on the browned almonds. Cut pineapple rings in half and arrange on top of sponge with the cherries in between them. Brush with apricot glaze, decorate edges with piped whipped cream. Serve chilled.

🥄 The slab sponge may be made 2 days in advance.

Two-tier wedding cake 1

This makes rather a shallow cake. If you prefer a deeper one use recipe 2. The basic method for all three cakes is the same: it has been placed at the end of the ingredients lists for easy reference. Cooking times and tins required have been listed after each ingredients list as these vary. Before embarking on your cake, gather together all necessary ingredients and equipment.

Ingredients:
2¼ lb. currants
12 oz. raisins
9 oz. sultanas
9 oz. cut mixed peel
4 oz. glacé cherries
3 oz. blanched almonds
3 oz. ground almonds
3¾ fl. oz. brandy
15 oz. self-raising flour
¼ teaspoonful salt
2 teaspoonfuls mixed spice
12 oz. butter or margarine
12 oz. soft brown sugar
7 eggs
3 tablespoonfuls warmed black treacle
1 tablespoonful coffee essence
grated rind 1 orange

Tins required:
9 inch and 6 inch square or 10 inch and 7 inch round

Cooking times:
large tier: 1 hour at 350°F., Gas mark 4, then 3 hours at 275°F., Gas mark 1
small tier: 1 hour at 350°F., Gas mark 4, then 1½ hours at 275°F., Gas mark 1

Two-tier wedding cake 2

Ingredients:
3½ lb. currants
1 lb. sultanas
1 lb. raisins
4 oz. cut mixed peel
8 oz. glacé cherries
4 oz. blanched almonds
4 oz. ground almonds
¼ pint brandy
1¾ lb. self-raising flour
½ teaspoonful salt
4 teaspoonfuls mixed spice
1¼ lb. butter or margarine
1¼ lb. soft brown sugar
16 eggs
2 tablespoonfuls warmed black treacle
2 teaspoonfuls coffee essence
grated rind 2 oranges

Tins required:
10 inch and 7 inch square or 11 inch and 8 inch round

Cooking times:
large tier: 1 hour at 350°F., Gas mark 4, then 5 hours at 275°F., Gas mark 1
small tier: 1 hour at 350°F., Gas mark 4, then 3½ hours at 275°F., Gas mark 1

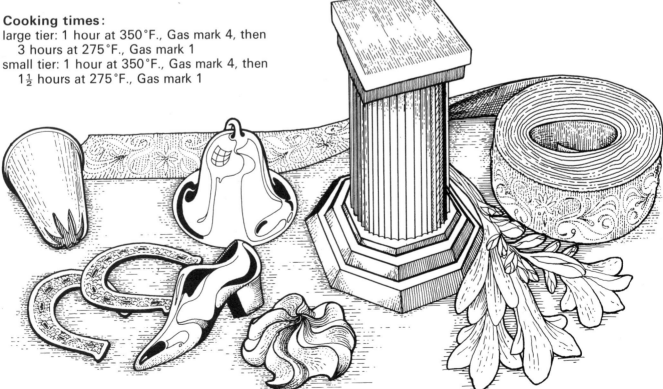

Three-tier wedding cake

Ingredients:

large tier	middle tier	small tier	
2½ lb.	1 lb.	8 oz.	currants
1¼ lb.	8 oz.	4 oz.	sultanas
10 oz.	4 oz.	2 oz.	raisins
5 oz.	2 oz.	1 oz.	glacé cherries
5 oz.	2 oz.	1 oz.	cut mixed peel
4 oz.	1½ oz.	½ oz.	ground almonds
4 oz.	1½ oz.	½ oz.	blanched almonds
5 Tbsp	2 Tbsp	1 Tbsp	brandy
1 lb. 9 oz.	10 oz.	5 oz.	self-raising flour
½ tsp	large pinch	pinch	salt
2 tsp	1 tsp	½ tsp	spice
1¼ lb.	8 oz.	4 oz.	butter
1¼ lb.	8 oz.	4 oz.	soft brown sugar
15	6	3	eggs
2 tsp	1 tsp	½ tsp	treacle
2 tsp	1 tsp	½ tsp	coffee essence
½	¼	a little	orange rind
½	¼	a little	lemon rind

Tins required:
11 inch, 8 inch and 6 inch square or 12 inch,
   9 inch and 7 inch round

Cooking times:
large tier: 1 hour at 350°F., Gas mark 4, then
   5½ hours at 275°F., Gas mark 1
middle tier: 1 hour at 350°F., Gas mark 4, then
   4 hours at 275°F., Gas mark 1
small tier: 1 hour at 350°F., Gas mark 4, then
   2 hours at 275°F., Gas mark 1

Basic method of making wedding cake
Clean the fruit carefully; chop cherries and nuts. Mix all the dried fruit in a large bowl, pour over the brandy, mix well and cover with foil; leave overnight. Grease tins and double-line with greaseproof paper. Prepare mixture by the creaming method, see page 19, and divide between the tins; smooth level. Bake as directed, covering the cakes with greaseproof paper when the tops have browned. Allow to cool in the tins overnight.
Peel off the greaseproof paper, wrap in fresh grease-proof paper and foil. Store in a cool, dry place for 6—8 weeks before applying the almond paste—apply the paste about 12 days before the cake is required. For quantities of almond paste and royal icing and directions on how to apply these see pages 52—55.

The cake mixture may be made up one day, kept covered in a cool place overnight and baked the next day. If you wish to keep a tier of the cake for future use—a christening or first wedding anniversary for example—always renew the almond paste and icing before the cake's second appearance.

Christening parties

Mid-afternoon is the customary time for the ceremony and as this is usually a less formal affair than the traditional wedding, all those present are usually invited back to tea. Whether you offer tea first and champagne after, vice versa or both together is a matter of taste, but a tea-table groaning with goodies is essential. Below we offer suggestions for a traditional christening tea: the recipes will be found on the following pages. Unless you expect a great many guests, pick a selection of these and allow, say, three savoury and two sweet items per person. The drinks section on page 113 will advise you on how much tea and champagne to allow per person— don't forget to have a supply of milk and squash on hand for the children.

Sausage rolls, see page 29
Selection of open sandwiches
Cheesy oat biscuits
Stuffed eggs with buttered brown bread
Savoury scones
Chicken and walnut tartlets
Coffee cream buns
Sponge drops
Strawberry and grape rosettes
Plain and coffee meringues
Frosted christening cake

Tea, see page 114
Champagne, see page 113
Squash or Summer punch, see page 114
Milk

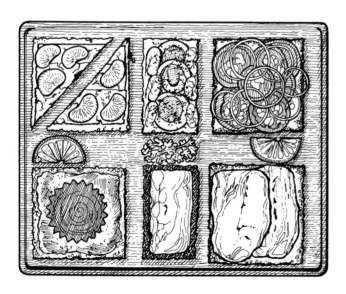

The picture on previous page shows plain and coffee meringues, page 84; frosted christening cake, page 85

Open sandwiches

white bread
brown bread
volkornbrot or pumpernickel (both these may be obtained from some supermarkets and some bakers, and are conveniently pre-sliced)
butter

Fillings:
liver pâté, decorated with drained beetroot
blue cheese, thinly sliced, with mandarin orange segments
rare roast beef, thinly sliced, with horseradish sauce, sprinkled with paprika pepper
tomato slices and watercress, topped with a raw onion ring
roast pork, thinly sliced, with cranberry jelly
eggs, hardboiled and sliced, mixed with shrimps and a little mayonnaise, see page 25
cooked ham, thinly sliced, spread with mustard and rolled up
sardines sprinkled with sieved hardboiled egg yolk

Butter generously and arrange the fillings attractively on top; cover with polythene film or aluminium foil to keep the sandwiches fresh and moist.

Cheesy oat biscuits

makes about 3 dozen:
6 oz. plain flour
½ teaspoonful dry mustard
¼ teaspoonful salt
¼ teaspoonful pepper
4 oz. porage oats
4 oz. butter or margarine
4 oz. dry cheese, finely grated
1 egg, beaten

Garnish:
cream cheese
paprika pepper
parsley
stuffed olives, sliced

Prepare by the rubbing-in method, see page 19, adding enough beaten egg to make a stiff dough. Roll out thinly and cut into rounds with a 2½-inch plain cutter. Place on greased baking trays and prick well. Bake for 15 minutes at 375°F., Gas mark 5. Leave to cool.
To garnish: spread with a little cream cheese, dust with paprika pepper and top some with a sprig of parsley and some with a slice of stuffed olive.

These may be prepared several days in advance and garnished on the day of the party. Store in an airtight tin or wrap in foil.

Stuffed eggs

12 eggs, hardboiled

Filling:
1 x 3-oz. packet cream cheese
2 teaspoonfuls French mustard
2 tablespoonfuls mayonnaise
salt; pepper

Garnish:
watercress

Cut eggs in half lengthways, place yolks in a bowl. Add filling ingredients to yolks and beat until smooth. Pipe or spoon mixture into the egg whites, arrange on a platter with sprigs of watercress. Cover with polythene film or aluminium foil until needed. Serve with thinly sliced buttered brown bread.

Savoury scones

Prepare a batch of cheese scones, see page 56, using 1 lb. flour etc. When cool, split and spread with 1 of the following spreads:

Gherkin
Soften 4 oz. butter, beat in 1 teaspoonful chopped capers and 1 teaspoonful chopped gherkins; add a little pepper.

Liver pâté
Soften 2 oz. butter, beat in 4 oz. liver pâté or liver sausage, season with salt and pepper.

Cheese
Soften 4 oz. butter, beat in 2 oz. cheese, finely grated, and $\frac{1}{2}$ teaspoonful made mustard.

Egg
Mix 2 oz. softened butter with 3 chopped hardboiled eggs. Season well and bind with a little mayonnaise. Add chopped chives if liked.
Garnish with gherkin fans, tomato slices cut in four, cocktail onions or mustard and cress.

Chicken and walnut tartlets

shortcrust pastry using 8 oz. flour etc., see page 16

Filling:
6 oz. cooked chicken, finely diced
2 oz. walnuts, broken up
6 tablespoonfuls mayonnaise, see page 25

Grease 24 deep patty tins. Roll out pastry thinly and cut into rounds a little larger than the patty tins; re-roll the trimmings and make further rounds. Line the patty tins, pressing the pastry down firmly. Bake for 10 minutes at 400°F., Gas mark 6. Leave to cool. Mix together the filling ingredients, place a little of the

mixture in each pastry case and dust with paprika pepper.

The tartlets may be prepared up to 1 week beforehand. Store in an airtight tin or in aluminium foil. Fill when required.

Cheese nuts

2 oz. self-raising flour
pinch salt
pinch pepper
2 oz. ground almonds
1 oz. blanched almonds, finely chopped
1 oz. cheese, finely grated
2½ oz. butter
1 tablespoonful beaten egg
paprika pepper

Mix together flour, salt, pepper, almonds and cheese. Rub in the butter and add sufficient egg to make a stiff dough. Knead lightly and roll out on a floured board. Cut into small rounds and place on greased baking trays. Bake for 10–15 minutes at 400°F., Gas mark 6.
Cool on a wire tray, then sprinkle with paprika pepper.

Devils on horseback

24 prunes
chutney
12 rashers streaky bacon

Soak the prunes overnight; drain well. Remove stones and fill prunes with a little chutney. Remove the rinds from the bacon rashers and cut each rasher in half. Wrap each prune in a piece of bacon and grill, turning once, until the bacon is crisp. Serve hot or cold.

Coffee cream buns

makes about 2 dozen:
half quantity choux pastry using 2 oz. self-raising flour etc., see page 18, omitting the sugar
coffee glacé icing using 12 oz. icing sugar etc., see page 51

Filling:
1 oz. plain flour
2 oz. caster sugar
1 egg
1 egg yolk
½ pint milk
few drops vanilla essence

Prepare as for Cream buns, see page 37, but use about ½ teaspoonful mixture only for each bun.
To make the custard filling: blend flour, sugar, egg and egg yolk, beat until creamy. Heat the milk, pour the hot milk on to the egg mixture, mix well and return to the saucepan. Bring to the boil, stirring all the time, simmer for 3 minutes. Add vanilla essence. Pour into a small bowl, cover with wet greaseproof paper and allow to cool. Split buns when cool, fill with custard filling and ice.

Buns and filling may be prepared the day before: leave the buns on a wire cooling tray covered with a tea-towel: refresh in a hot oven when required.

Sponge drops

makes about 2 dozen:
6 oz. self-raising flour
pinch salt
4 eggs
6 oz. caster sugar

Filling:
whipped cream
raspberry jam

Grease 2–3 baking trays and dust with flour. Prepare mixture in 2 batches (each using 3 oz. flour, 2 eggs, 3 oz. sugar) by the whisking method, see page 19. Put teaspoonfuls of the mixture neatly on the baking trays. Bake for 5–7 minutes at 425°F., Gas mark 7, second and middle shelf. Remove from the baking trays while warm. When cool sandwich with a little whipped cream, see page 51, and raspberry jam.

Strawberry and grape rosettes

makes about 20:
Viennese rosettes using 8 oz. flour etc., see page 44

Decoration:
½ pint double cream
2 tablespoonfuls milk
2 small punnets strawberries
8 oz. green and black grapes

When required whip the cream and milk until soft peaks form. Peel paper cases off and place a little cream on each rosette. Place a strawberry on some of the cakes and a black and a green grape on the remainder.

The rosettes may be prepared 2–3 days in advance and decorated when required.

Plain and coffee meringues

makes about 18:
3 egg whites
6 oz. caster sugar
2 teaspoonfuls instant coffee

Cover 2–3 baking trays with greaseproof paper: do not grease the trays or the paper. Whisk egg whites until very stiff. Gradually whisk in half the sugar, then fold in the remainder. Divide mixture into 2. Put half into a forcing bag fitted with a star nozzle and pipe in small swirls on to the prepared baking trays or place small teaspoonfuls of mixture on to the baking trays shaping each neatly. Fold instant coffee into the remaining mixture and pipe or place on to baking trays. Bake for 1½–2 hours, depending on size, at

250°F., Gas mark ½, middle shelf or lower. Peel off the paper and allow to cool. When required sandwich together with a little whipped cream, see page 51.

The meringues may be made up to 10 days in advance: store in an airtight tin or polythene container.

The meringue mixture may be piped into rounds for Meringue baskets. Pipe or shape the meringue into rounds on the greaseproof paper. Pipe round the edges of the round to form baskets. Bake as for plain meringues until crisp and dry. The baskets may be filled with fresh soft fruit, canned drained fruit or a mixture of fruit mixed with whipped cream.

The baskets should not be filled with the fruit mixture too far in advance of serving as it will make the meringue soft.

Frosted christening cake

8 oz. butter or margarine
8 oz. caster sugar
8 oz. plain flour
pinch salt
3 eggs
4 oz. ground almonds
12 oz. sultanas
4 oz. glacé cherries, chopped

Frosting:
1 lb. icing sugar, sieved
1 egg white
juice ½ lemon
4 tablespoonfuls boiling water

To decorate:
10-inch round cake board
artificial flowers

Grease and line an 8-inch round cake tin. Prepare mixture by the creaming method, see page 19, place in prepared tin and smooth level. Bake for 3¼ hours at 275°F., Gas mark 1. When cold wrap in grease-proof paper and foil and store for a week to mellow. The day before the cake is required, place it on the cake board and prepare the frosting: place all the ingredients in a bowl and whisk until the mixture stands in peaks. Spread over the cake and swirl attractively.

A charming decoration may be made by arranging tiny artificial flowers round the bottom of the cake. Use a mixture of white and either pink, blue or lemon flowers. Cut the stalks to about 1 inch in length and push into the frosting. Alternatively, place a small cradle or stork on the top of the cake after the frosting has set slightly.

Rum truffles

4 oz. cake crumbs
4 oz. caster sugar
4 oz. ground almonds
2 tablespoonfuls rum
sieved apricot jam, warmed
chocolate vermicelli

Mix together the cake crumbs, caster sugar and ground almonds. Add the rum and sufficient apricot jam to bind the mixture. Roll into 24 balls and allow to harden. Brush with a little apricot jam and toss in chocolate vermicelli. Serve in paper sweet cases.

Chocolate clusters

8 oz. plain chocolate
6 oz. raisins
3 oz. walnuts, chopped

Melt the chocolate in a basin over hot water. Stir in the raisins and walnuts. Place teaspoonfuls of the mixture into paper sweet cases and allow to set in a cool dry place.

Children's parties

These fall into two main categories: tots and teenagers. Each is completely different in every aspect except one—the need for festive food. For young children tea is always the highlight of the occasion (accompanied, perhaps, by a small but gaily-wrapped present at each child's place or a mound of crackers decoratively arranged in the centre of the table). You will find, perhaps to your surprise, that even the youngest of children are often particularly partial to savoury items. Small cocktail sausages on coloured sticks, for example, are always a great favourite and usually run out long before the richer sweet concoctions. Older children may appear less interested in food than their younger brothers and sisters, but by the end of the evening they will certainly have done it justice.

Such appreciation makes catering a particular pleasure and children frequently derive as much enjoyment from preparing the party as from actually participating. With these things in mind we have included food for youngsters and teenagers; this section is followed by a collection of recipes, specially selected, which children can cook themselves. Of course, the three sections overlap and your children will almost certainly have their own ideas on the subject. . . .

Drinks

A selection of children's party drinks will be found in the drinks section on pages 114–116. Older children may prefer the non-alcoholic Summer punch, page 114, or perhaps the Cider cup, page 113. Be sure to have a supply of well-chilled milk in the refrigerator—you will be surprised how many children, of all ages, prefer it to anything else.

Sandwich selection

For young children make sandwiches from a selection of small finger rolls, soft rolls halved, brown and white bread. Choose from the following suggested fillings:

Banana butter
Spread the bread or rolls with peanut butter instead of butter, fill with thinly sliced bananas tossed in lemon juice and sugar.

Bacon and egg
Grill streaky bacon until crisp, cool and crumble finely. Mix with scrambled egg, seasoned with onion salt.

Cheese and ham
Mix cottage cheese with finely chopped ham.

Cream cheese and jam
Spread the bread with cream cheese instead of butter and top with strawberry jam.

Cheese and pickle
Mix grated cheese with a little sweet pickle.

Crispy peanut
Spread the bread or rolls with crunchy peanut butter and fill with crushed potato crisps.

Nuts and honey
Spread the bread or rolls with butter and thick honey and sprinkle with chopped walnuts.

Ham and pineapple
Mix chopped ham with finely chopped pineapple and a little made mustard.

For older children make open sandwiches: use a mixture of cream cracker biscuits and rye bread, butter thickly and arrange toppings:

Salami and sweet pickle
Sliced salami and sweet pickle, garnished with a slice of hardboiled egg.

Bacon
Rashers of bacon, de-rinded, grilled until crisp, garnished with crisp lettuce.

Chicken and orange
Thinly sliced chicken with orange segments and watercress.

Continental
Cottage cheese with sliced tomato and black olives.

For more ideas, see page 82.

Savoury dips

Serve these with a selection of small plain or cheese biscuits, pieces of celery or carrot. To make a more substantial dish, serve grilled chipolata sausages or tiny meat balls: mix 1 lb. finely minced beef with salt and pepper, make into tiny meat balls and fry gently for 8–10 minutes turning occasionally until brown and cooked through; drain well. These are also very good served with Tomato sauce or Barbecue sauce, see page 24.

Cheese and onion
8 oz. cottage cheese mixed with 3 spring onions, finely chopped, and seasoned with pepper.

Cheese and onion dip; cheese and shrimp dip; hot cheese dip

Cheese and ham

8 oz. cottage cheese mixed with 2 oz. ham, finely chopped, and 1 tablespoonful green pepper, also finely chopped.

Cheese and shrimp

8 oz. cottage cheese mixed with 1 small can shrimps, drained and chopped.

Hot cheese

½ pint white sauce, see page 22, mixed with 6 oz. cheese, grated, and 1 teaspoonful French mustard, reheated until almost boiling. Serve this one immediately!

Crispy tartlets

shortcrust pastry using 8 oz. flour etc., see page 16

Filling:
1 oz. flour
1 oz. butter or margarine
½ pint milk
salt; pepper
4 eggs, hardboiled and chopped
2 small packets potato crisps

Grease 24 patty tins or individual tartlet tins. Roll out pastry thinly and line the tins. Make a white sauce, see page 22, with the flour, fat and milk; season to taste. Stir in the eggs and place a spoonful in each pastry case. Crush the crisps, sprinkle over tartlets and bake for 15 minutes at 400°F., Gas mark 6.

Savoury cheese tartlets

shortcrust pastry using 8 oz. flour etc., see page 16

Filling:
8 oz. streaky bacon
2 eggs
salt; pepper
4–5 tomatoes, skinned and sliced
6 slices processed cheese

Grease 24 patty tins or individual tartlet tins. Roll out pastry thinly and line the tins. Chop the bacon and fry gently for 5 minutes. Drain and divide between the pastry cases. Beat the eggs with a little seasoning and pour over the bacon. Top each tartlet with a slice of tomato and a quarter of a slice of cheese. Bake for 15 minutes at 400°F., Gas mark 6. If liked garnish with parsley sprigs.

Sausage pinwheels

Base:
8 oz. self-raising flour
pinch salt
pinch dried mustard
2 oz. butter or margarine
2 oz. cheese, finely grated
6–7 tablespoonfuls milk

Fillings:
8 oz. sausagemeat
1 tablespoonful tomato purée
1 teaspoonful Worcestershire sauce
$\frac{1}{2}$ teaspoonful salt
$\frac{1}{2}$ teaspoonful pepper
1 small egg, beaten

Prepare base by the rubbing-in method, see page 19. Knead lightly and roll out to an oblong approximately 14 by 9 inches. Mix together ingredients for the filling and spread over the pastry to within $\frac{1}{2}$ inch of the edge. Roll up like a Swiss roll, from the long edge, damping the edge to seal firmly. Trim the ends and cut roll in half, cut each half-roll into 12 slices. Place cut-side down on greased baking trays and bake for 15 minutes at 425°F., Gas mark 7. Serve hot or cold.

Hamburgers with variations

2 lb. lean minced beef
1 onion, peeled and grated
1 teaspoonful Worcestershire sauce
salt; black pepper

Toppings:
onion rings; tomato ketchup; fruit sauce; grated cheese; sliced tomatoes; French mustard; sweet pickle; pineapple rings; rings of green pepper; pickled onions and gherkins

Combine all the ingredients, divide into 16 x 2-oz. portions. Shape into flat cakes with wet hands. Fry in moderately hot shallow fat or oil for about 4 minutes on each side. Drain well.
Serve in buttered soft rolls with a selection of toppings served separately, so that the children can choose their own favourites.

Opposite: Toffee apples, page 94
Below: Hamburgers

Sausage cornets

A simple but popular idea for parties is to serve sausages and chips or potato crisps in greaseproof paper bags or cornets. To make the cornets take a 14-inch square of greaseproof paper, fold diagonally to make a triangle, follow the directions for making piping bags, see page 54. Secure at the join with clear adhesive tape. Allow 2–4 chipolata sausages per head, cook in a moderate oven for 20–25 minutes. Blanch the chips for 5 minutes in moderately hot deep fat and drain well: this may be done on the morning of the party. When required brown in hot fat for 2–3 minutes, drain well, place a portion in each paper bag or cornet and top with sausages: let each child help himself to tomato ketchup or fruit sauce. If crisps are used heat these through in the oven for 5 minutes while the sausages are cooking.

Barbecued beans

1 onion, peeled and chopped
1 tablespoonful oil
1 x 20-oz. can baked beans
salt; pepper
½ teaspoonful brown sugar
1 teaspoonful vinegar
few drops Tabasco sauce
4 tablespoonfuls tomato ketchup
6 rashers bacon, de-rinded and chopped

Fry onion in oil for 5 minutes. Stir in all the other ingredients except the bacon. Pour mixture into a greased ovenproof dish, sprinkle with bacon. Bake, uncovered, for 25 minutes at 375°F., Gas mark 5.

Hawaiian beans

1 x 10-oz. can pineapple rings
1 x 20-oz. can baked beans
brown sugar

Chop 3 of the pineapple rings; mix with the beans and place in greased ovenproof dish. Cut each of the remaining 3 rings into 4 and place on top of the beans. Sprinkle with brown sugar and bake for 25 minutes at 375°F., Gas mark 5.

Serve Barbecued beans and Hawaiian beans with crisp rolls or French bread. To reheat the bread, wrap it closely in aluminium foil and place in a hot oven, 425°F., Gas mark 7, for 10–15 minutes.

Salad baskets

allow per person:
1 bread roll
1–2 teaspoonfuls sandwich spread
1 hardboiled egg
1 tomato, skinned
mustard and cress

Slice the top off the roll; remove some of the crumb and spread the inside with sandwich spread. Chop the egg and tomato and spoon into the roll. Garnish with mustard and cress and replace the top.

Cheese whirls

4 oz. self-raising flour
pinch salt
pinch pepper
2 oz. cheese, grated
2 oz. butter or margarine
yolk of 1 egg
about 1 tablespoonful cold water
meat or vegetable extract

Mix flour, salt, pepper and cheese. Rub in fat and mix to a firm dough with egg yolk and water. Roll out to a 12-inch square. Spread with meat or vegetable extract and roll up like a Swiss roll. Cut into ½ inch slices and lay, cut side down on greased baking trays. Bake for 10–12 minutes at 400°F., Gas mark 6.

Crispy sandwiches

allow per person:
2 slices from a large loaf
cream cheese or butter
1 slice ham
little made mustard
¼ oz. butter
1 tablespoonful oil

Spread one slice of bread with cream cheese or butter, cover with a slice of ham, spread with mustard. Put the second slice of bread on top, trim off the crusts and cut in half to make two triangles. Heat the butter and oil and fry the sandwiches for 2 minutes on each side, until crisp and brown. Drain on absorbent paper.

Jelly oranges

1 orange table jelly
1 lime table jelly
6 large oranges

Make up the jellies as directed on the packet. Wash the oranges, cut in half and carefully squeeze out the juice, making sure the skins remain whole. Remove the orange pulp with a teaspoon. Just before the jellies set, pour them into the orange shells. Allow to set overnight, then cut each half into 2 with a sharp knife.

Use the orange juice in a party drink, see page 114.

Jelly fingers

Swiss roll sponge mixture, see page 50
1 red table jelly
1 x 8-oz. can fruit cocktail, drained

Jelly oranges

Grease the Swiss roll tin and line with greaseproof paper to a height of approximately $2\frac{1}{2}$ inches. Bake the mixture as directed, but leave it in the tin to cool. Make up the jelly and just before it sets add the fruit cocktail. Pour mixture over the sponge and allow to set overnight. Peel off the greaseproof paper and cut into fingers with a knife dipped in hot water.

Trifle-in-a-trifling

1 x 7-inch Victoria sandwich, see page 45
3 oz. plain chocolate
$\frac{1}{2}$ pint milk
3 egg yolks
1 tablespoonful sugar
coloured sugar strands for decoration

Cut sponge into 8 and crumble into 8 small glass or waxed paper dishes. Gently heat chocolate and milk until the chocolate dissolves. Stir in the egg yolks and heat gently, stirring, for 3—4 minutes—do not allow to boil. Remove from the heat, add the sugar and divide the mixture evenly between the 8 dishes; allow to cool. Before serving, sprinkle with coloured sugar strands.

Chocolate peppermint bars

Sponge:
4 oz. butter or margarine
8 oz. soft brown sugar
4 oz. self-raising flour
pinch salt
1½ oz. cocoa
2 eggs

Topping:
6–8 oz. chocolate peppermint creams

Grease a deep 11 by 7 inch Swiss roll tin. Prepare sponge mixture by the creaming method, see page 19, softening the fat well to make this easier. Spread evenly in the tin and bake for 30 minutes at 375°F., Gas mark 5. When cooked, remove from the oven and arrange the chocolate peppermint creams on top. Return to the oven for about 30 seconds until the chocolates have melted then spread over with a knife. When cold, cut into fingers.

Flapjacks

6 oz. butter or margarine
4 oz. demerara sugar
2 tablespoonfuls golden syrup
few drops vanilla essence
8 oz. porage oats

Grease an 11 by 7 inch Swiss roll tin. Melt the fat, sugar and syrup very gently until the fat melts. Stir in the vanilla essence and oats. Spread evenly into the tin and bake for 15–20 minutes at 375°F., Gas mark 5. Cut into fingers and remove from tin while warm.

Toffee bars

Biscuit base:
6 oz. plain flour
4 oz. butter or margarine
2 oz. caster sugar

Toffee:
1 small can condensed milk
4 oz. butter or margarine
2 oz. soft brown sugar
few drops vanilla essence

Topping:
6 oz. plain chocolate, melted

Grease an 11 by 7 inch Swiss roll tin. Prepare the biscuit mixture by the rubbing-in method, see page 19. Press evenly in to the tin and bake for 20 minutes at 350°F., Gas mark 4. Meanwhile, heat the con-

densed milk, fat and sugar until the sugar melts and cook for 5 minutes, stirring all the time; add vanilla essence. Pour toffee over the cooled biscuit base, spread evenly. When cold, cover with melted chocolate and leave in a cool, dry place to set. Cut into fingers.

Toffee apples

12 eating apples
a little cooking oil
1 lb. granulated sugar
2 teaspoonfuls golden syrup
½ pint water
large pinch cream of tartar

To hold:
12 wooden skewers

To decorate:
coloured cellophane

Wash and dry apples; stick a skewer in each. Oil a baking tray. Put sugar, syrup, water and cream of tartar into a heavy-based saucepan, heat gently until sugar dissolves then boil until the mixture is golden brown (about 20 minutes). Remove from heat. Test the toffee mixture by dropping a little in cold water: if it is ready it will form a very hard ball. Dip each apple in the toffee then place on the greased baking tray to set. Once set, wrap in gaily coloured cellophane paper.

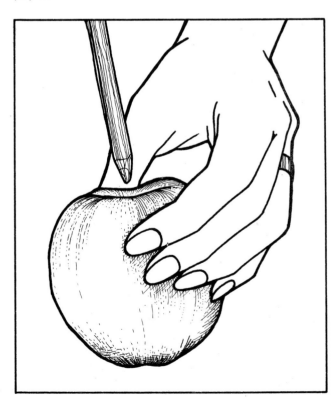

Cooking children can do themselves

Cherry scones

8 oz. self-raising flour
pinch salt
2 oz. butter or margarine
1 oz. caster sugar
¼ pint milk
glacé cherries
a little milk for brushing

Mix the flour and salt, rub in the butter and stir in the sugar. Add the milk and mix with a fork to make a dough. Knead lightly on a floured board and roll out until about ¼ inch thick. Cut into rounds with a plain cutter about 2¼ inches across. Place half the rounds on a greased baking tray and brush them with milk. Put a glacé cherry in the centre of each round and cover with another scone round to make a 'sandwich'. Press the edges down firmly. Bake for 10–12 minutes at 425°F., Gas mark 7, on the second shelf.

Orange drizzle cake

4 oz. butter or margarine
4 oz. caster sugar
grated rind 1 orange
2 eggs
4 oz. self-raising flour
pinch salt

Topping:
juice 1 orange
1 oz. caster sugar

Grease a 9 by 4 inch loaf tin and line the base with greaseproof paper. Cream the butter and sugar with the orange rind until light and fluffy. Beat in the eggs, one at a time, adding a tablespoonful of flour with each. Fold in the remaining flour and salt. Place the mixture into the prepared tin and smooth level. Bake for 35–40 minutes at 350°F., Gas mark 4. Place the orange juice and sugar into a small saucepan, heat gently until the sugar dissolves: bring to the boil. Pour the mixture over the hot cake while it is still in the tin. Remove the cake from the tin before it cools completely.

Yogurt jellies

1 raspberry table jelly
½ pint water
3 x 5-fl. oz. cartons raspberry yogurt

Dissolve the jelly in a little hot water and make up to ½ pint with cold water. Allow to cool but not set. Empty the yogurt into a bowl and stir in the cooled jelly, making sure it is well mixed. Pour into 6 small dishes and allow to set.

Chocolate crunchy biscuits

5 oz. plain flour
pinch salt
1 oz. cocoa
4 oz. butter or margarine
2 oz. caster sugar
1 tablespoonful milk
a few drops vanilla essence
1 oz. demerara sugar

Sieve flour, salt and cocoa into a bowl. Rub in the butter and add the caster sugar, milk and vanilla essence. Knead well to make a smooth dough. Roll into a sausage shape about 10 inches long. Sprinkle the demerara sugar on to a piece of greaseproof paper and roll the biscuit dough in the sugar until the 'sausage' is coated, then cut it into slices just under ½ inch thick and place on 2 greased baking trays. Bake for 15–20 minutes at 350°F., Gas mark 4.

Party mice

Biscuits:
3 oz. plain flour
pinch salt
2 oz. butter or margarine
1 oz. caster sugar

To decorate:
1 carton chocolate spread
canned pear halves, drained
currants
split almonds
liquorice strips

Mix the flour and salt; rub in the butter and add the sugar. Knead well to form a smooth dough. Roll out thinly on a floured board and cut into rounds with a 3-inch cutter. Place on a greased baking tray and prick with a fork. Bake for about 30 minutes at 300°F., Gas mark 2, until the biscuits are a pale golden brown. To decorate, spread the biscuits thinly with chocolate spread. Dry the pear halves with kitchen paper and place one on each biscuit, cut-side down. Decorate with currant 'eyes' and 'nose', almond 'ears' and liquorice 'tails'.

Almond walnut loaf

4 oz. butter or margarine
6 oz. caster sugar
2 eggs
$\frac{1}{2}$ teaspoonful almond essence
$\frac{1}{2}$ teaspoonful vanilla essence
6 oz. self-raising flour
2 oz. ground almonds
2 tablespoonfuls milk
1 oz. walnuts, chopped

Grease a 9 by 5 inch loaf tin and line the base with greaseproof paper. Prepare the mixture by the creaming method, see page 19. Transfer mixture to the tin and smooth level. Bake at 350°F., Gas mark 4 for 50 minutes. Allow to cool for a few minutes before turning out of the tin.
Cool on a wire tray.

Mandarin jelly cake

4 oz. butter or margarine
4 oz. caster sugar
2 eggs
4 oz. self-raising flour
pinch salt
1 x 11-oz. can mandarin oranges, drained
  reserving juice
1 orange table jelly
$\frac{1}{2}$ pint boiling water

Grease an ovenproof dish. Prepare the mixture by the creaming method, see page 19, adding the drained mandarin oranges. Place into dish, smooth level. Bake for 30 minutes at 375°F., Gas mark 5. Meanwhile dissolve the jelly in $\frac{1}{2}$ pint boiling water, add mandarin juice.
Pour jelly over cake while hot.
Allow to set before serving.

Golden apricot crumble

1 x 15-oz. can apricot halves
2 oz. butter or margarine
2 teaspoonfuls golden syrup
2 oz. demerara or granulated sugar
3 oz. porage oats

Open the can of apricots and pour off about half the juice into a small jug: keep this to serve with the pudding. Arrange the apricots cut-side down in a small ovenproof dish. Melt the butter and syrup over a gentle heat. Add the sugar and mix well. Remove from the heat and stir in the oats. Spread the mixture over the apricots and bake for 25 minutes at 375°F., Gas mark 5.

Truffles

1 oz. butter
3 tablespoonfuls milk
1½ oz. caster sugar
2 tablespoonfuls cocoa
2 oz. porage oats
2 oz. desiccated coconut
2 tablespoonfuls raisins

To decorate:
desiccated coconut or chocolate vermicelli

Heat the butter and milk until the butter melts. Stir in the sugar and cocoa powder. Add the other ingredients and mix well. Allow the mixture to cool, then make it into about 20 small balls. Roll these in coconut or chocolate vermicelli if liked. Place in paper sweet cases and allow to set.

Orange creams

1 egg white
about **14 oz.** icing sugar, sieved
finely grated rind 1 orange
2 tablespoonfuls orange juice

Beat the egg white lightly with a fork then gradually work in the other ingredients to make a stiff dough. Roll out the mixture on sugared greaseproof paper until it is about ¼ inch thick and cut into small rounds. Arrange on a tray and allow to dry.

Chocolate fudge

4 oz. plain chocolate
2 oz. butter
4 tablespoonfuls evaporated milk
1 lb. icing sugar, sieved

Melt the chocolate and butter in a bowl over hot water (do not allow the water to boil). Stir in the evaporated milk and work in the icing sugar. Press the mixture into a greased tin, approximately 7 by 7 inches. Allow the mixture to set then cut it into squares.

Special tomato soup

1 x 15-oz. can tomato soup
1 x 8-oz. can baked beans
4 oz. cheese, grated

Heat the soup and beans together until piping hot. Ladle into 4 warmed soup dishes and sprinkle with grated cheese. Serve with crusty rolls and butter.

Pasta supper dish

6 oz. macaroni or pasta shapes
½ oz. butter
4 tablespoonfuls tomato sauce
1 small packet processed cheese slices

Cook the macaroni in boiling salted water until tender but not mushy (about 10 minutes). Drain and return to the saucepan. Add the butter and tomato sauce. Mix well then place in a greased ovenproof dish. Cut each of the cheese slices into 4 triangles and arrange on top of the macaroni. Grill until the cheese melts and serve piping hot.

Super baked potatoes

4 large potatoes
4 rashers bacon
1 small onion
1 oz. butter
salt; pepper

Scrub the potatoes and prick them with a fork. Bake for 1¼ hours at 375°F., Gas mark 5. Meanwhile de-rind and cut up the bacon with a pair of scissors. Peel and chop the onion: fry gently with the bacon for 5 minutes. When the potatoes are cooked, cut them in 2 lengthways and scoop out the centres into a bowl. Add the cooked bacon and onion and the butter: mix well and season to taste. Pile this mixture back into the potato shells and bake for a further 15 minutes.

Dinner parties and buffets

A first dinner party is nearly always a bit of an ordeal. Whether you're a brand new wife in a new (or at least unfamiliar) kitchen, surrounded by brand new pots and pans and a husband who thinks you're perfect, or a carefree but career-minded single girl, you will be expected, practically overnight, to have acquired all the domestic arts which your grandmother probably spent years learning at her mother's knee. And first dinner parties so very often seem to include your husband's employer or his parents or someone equally special whom you wish to impress. Small wonder that this occasion has the reputation of being something of an ordeal for the hostess.

We can't offer experience overnight, of course, but we **can** give you the benefit of our own experience to help with your first tentative efforts and avoid major disasters. To do this we have designed the section around complete menus, all of them planned and tested down to the last detail. To make things even easier we have devised menus for two people, menus for four, for six—and buffet parties for twelve. By a little simple arithmetic the menus can obviously be altered to accommodate any number of people, but at first it is best to leave nothing to chance and keep the catering as simple as possible. All advance preparation is clearly marked (look for the small spoon sign) to avoid last-minute marathons; advice on drinks and general hints will be found at the beginning of 'Cooking for special occasions'.

More experienced cooks won't need such help, of course (though if time's at a premium they may be glad of it), but we hope they will enjoy the recipes themselves and that the section will provide them with a source of new ideas and menus to try out.

The picture on previous page shows chilled cucumber soup, page 103

Menus for 2 people

Crab and coleslaw salad
Veal escalopes with ham and cheese
Ratatouille and mashed potatoes
Strawberry palmiers
Coffee

Crab and coleslaw salad

2 oz. white cabbage, shredded
1 small onion, peeled and grated
¼ green pepper, cored and thinly sliced
1 x 2-oz. can crab, flaked
4 tablespoonfuls mayonnaise, see page 25
salt; cayenne pepper

Combine all ingredients, pile into 2 glasses and serve chilled.

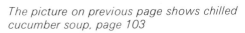 May be made in the morning and kept in the refrigerator.

Veal escalopes with ham and cheese

2 escalopes veal
1 oz. butter
2 thin slices lean bacon, de-rinded
2 thin slices gruyère cheese
2 tablespoonfuls single cream

Lightly brown the veal escalopes on both sides in the butter. Place in a shallow baking dish. Stretch bacon with the back of a knife, cut in half. Lay bacon on top of veal, cover with the cheese slices. Bake for 20 minutes at 400°F., Gas mark 6, then spoon over the cream and put back in the oven for a further 5 minutes.

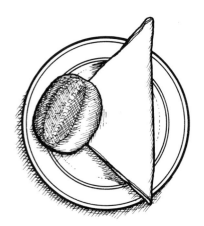

Ratatouille

1 onion, peeled and sliced
1 green pepper, cored and sliced
1 tablespoonful oil
1 oz. butter
1 small aubergine, sliced without peeling
2 courgettes, sliced without peeling
3 tomatoes, skinned, sliced or quartered and
   de-seeded
1 clove garlic, peeled and crushed
salt
freshly milled black pepper

Fry onion and pepper in heated oil and butter in a covered pan until soft (about 5 minutes). Add aubergine and courgettes and cook mixture together for 5 minutes. Add tomatoes, garlic and seasonings, stir well. Cover pan and simmer gently for about 30 minutes until tender.

Ratatouille may be made the night before the party or in the morning: reheat it in the oven whilst the veal is being cooked.

Mashed potatoes

¾–1 lb. potatoes
1 teaspoonful salt
pepper
knob butter
a little milk

Peel potatoes and cut up into even pieces if large. Cover with boiling water, add a teaspoonful of salt and cook gently until tender (20–25 minutes). Drain and mash, check the seasoning, add a little butter and milk and beat until fluffy.

Strawberry palmiers

4 oz. puff pastry
caster sugar
¼ pint double cream
4 oz. strawberries, hulled and sliced

If using frozen pastry, allow it to thaw out for 1½–2 hours. Roll out pastry thinly to a narrow oblong. Sprinkle with sugar, fold in either end to the centre, sprinkle with sugar. Repeat folds, sprinkle with sugar and fold over. Cut into 4 slices, press down slightly with the hand. Sprinkle sugar over the top and place on a wetted baking tray and bake for 15 minutes at 425°F., Gas mark 7, until golden. Place, top-side down, on a cooling tray. Whip the cream and when the palmiers are cold, sandwich 2 together with cream and strawberries in the centre. If liked sprinkle with more sugar.

The palmiers may be baked in the morning or the day before. In the latter case, re-crisp in the oven whilst the meal is being prepared and allow to cool. Fill just before dinner and keep in a cool place.

Coffee, see page 114.

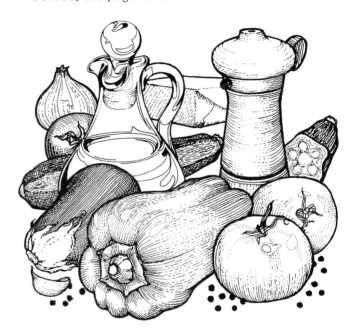

Asparagus quiche
Lobster thermidor
Mixed green salad
Fresh fruit salad
Coffee

Asparagus quiche

shortcrust pastry using 2 oz. flour etc., see page 16

Filling:
3 oz. canned asparagus tips, roughly chopped
4 stuffed green olives, sliced
1 tablespoonful single cream or top of milk
1 egg, beaten
salt; pepper

Roll out pastry and line 2 x 4-inch patty tins. Arrange asparagus on the base then add the sliced olives. Mix together the cream and egg, season lightly and pour into pastry cases. Bake for 20 minutes at 375°F., Gas mark 5, shelf above the centre.

May be made in the morning and served cold. Alternatively line the tins with pastry the night before, leave covered with a plastic bag or film, then fill and bake when required.

Above: Asparagus quiche, page 101
Below: Strawberry palmiers, page 101

Lobster thermidor

1 cooked lobster, split in half
1 oz. butter
1 tablespoonful oil
1 shallot, peeled and chopped
1 teaspoonful chopped parsley or pinch dried
   parsley
1 teaspoonful chopped tarragon or pinch dried
   tarragon
$\frac{1}{2}$ glass dry white wine
$\frac{1}{4}$ pint Béchamel sauce, see page 24
3 tablespoonfuls single cream
a little French mustard
salt; paprika pepper
2 tablespoonfuls Parmesan cheese
1 rounded tablespoonful browned breadcrumbs

Remove stomach and intestines from the lobster if
the fishmonger has not already done this. Take out
the flesh from the body, tail and claws and dice it.
Wash the shells and reserve for serving.
Melt the butter and oil, add shallot and herbs and
cook gently for a few minutes. Add the wine, increase the heat and cook rapidly to reduce by half.
Stir wine into the sauce gradually, add cream, lobster
meat, mustard and seasonings to taste and mix well.
Pour into the cleaned shells. Sprinkle with cheese
and crumbs and brown under the grill.

Mixed green salad

1 small lettuce
1 bunch watercress

French dressing:
4 tablespoonfuls salad oil
1–2 tablespoonfuls wine or cider vinegar
pinch salt and sugar
shake pepper
few drops Worcestershire sauce (optional)

Place all ingredients for dressing in a small bottle and shake well before use. Trim lettuce and remove stalks from watercress. Wash and dry. Put into the salad bowl, pour over dressing just before serving and toss well.

Dressing may be made in advance. Wash and lightly dry salad ingredients in the morning. Store in a plastic bag in the refrigerator and when required dry completely on a clean towel or roll of kitchen paper.

Fresh fruit salad

1 rosy apple
1 ripe pear
1 clementine or orange
2 oz. each black and white grapes
1 banana

Syrup:
2 oz. sugar
¼ pint water
strip lemon rind

To make syrup, dissolve sugar slowly in the water, add rind and boil for 2–3 minutes. Transfer to a bowl and leave to cool. Remove lemon rind.
Wash apple but do not peel. Cut into quarters, remove core and slice very thinly. Peel the pear, cut into quarters, remove core and cut each quarter in half again. Peel and remove all pith from orange or clementine, divide into segments. Cut grapes into half, remove pips using a fine skewer. As soon as each fruit is prepared add it to the syrup, coating well. Add peeled and sliced banana just before serving.

Syrup may be made the night before, and the fruit, apart from the banana, may be added in the morning.

Coffee, see page 114.

Menus for 4 people

**Chilled cucumber soup
Orange duck casserole
New potatoes and peas
Honey and nut fluff
Coffee**

Chilled cucumber soup

1 small onion, peeled and chopped
1 cucumber, washed and chopped, reserving a few slices for decoration
1 oz. butter
1 oz. plain flour
1 pint chicken stock
4 tablespoonfuls milk
salt
pepper
4 tablespoonfuls single cream

Make the soup following directions for Cream of vegetable soup, page 28. Chill. Stir in cream, garnish with the reserved cucumber slices.

May be made the day before, covered and stored in the refrigerator.

Orange duck casserole

1 medium duck (about **3½–4 lb.**) cut into 4
1–2 oz. butter
2 onions, peeled and sliced
2 carrots, peeled and sliced
½ oz. plain flour
⅓ pint water
½ pint inexpensive red wine
grated rind and juice 2 oranges
salt
pepper

Brown duck in 1 oz. heated butter, drain and place in a casserole. Add onions and carrots to fat and adding a little more if necessary, cook gently until golden. Stir in flour and cook for a minute. Gradually blend in water and wine, stir until sauce boils. Add rind and juice of oranges and season to taste. Pour sauce over duck, cover and cook for 1½ hours at 375°F., Gas mark 5, until tender.

New potatoes

1½ lb. new potatoes
salt
sprig mint

Cook as directed on page 108.

Peas

2 lb. peas or **1-lb.** packet frozen peas
a little salt
pinch sugar
sprig mint
knob butter

Prepare peas, cook in enough boiling water to cover, with a little salt, sugar and mint or cook frozen peas as directed. Drain, place in a serving dish with a little butter.

Honey and nut fluff

$\frac{1}{3}$ pint double cream
1 egg white
2 tablespoonfuls clear honey
2 oz. walnuts, chopped

Whisk cream and egg white together until fluffy and fairly stiff. Fold in honey and walnuts. Pile into glass dishes.

➤ May be made in the morning, covered lightly and kept in the refrigerator.

Coffee, see page 114.

Cottage cornets
Liver and kidneys in red wine
Noodles and courgettes
Flan panachie
Coffee

Cottage cornets

8 oz. cottage cheese
$\frac{1}{2}$ green pepper, cored and finely chopped
pinch cayenne pepper
4 thin slices ham
4 lettuce leaves and a little thinly sliced
    cucumber for garnish

Mix together the cheese and green pepper, adding a little cayenne pepper. Divide mixture between the slices of ham and roll up into cornets. Serve garnished with cucumber slices on a bed of lettuce.

Liver and kidneys in red wine

2 lambs' kidneys, cored and sliced
8 slices lamb's liver, washed and dried
2 oz. butter
4 oz. mushrooms, washed and sliced
2 onions, peeled and chopped
1 oz. plain flour
$\frac{1}{2}$ pint water
$\frac{1}{2}$ pint inexpensive red wine
1 tablespoonful tomato purée
salt
pepper
1 bay leaf

Lightly fry kidneys and liver in heated butter, drain and place in a casserole. Fry mushrooms and onions for a few minutes. Stir in flour and cook for 1 minute. Gradually blend in water and wine, bring to the boil, stirring all the time. Stir in tomato purée and season to taste. Add bay leaf to casserole and pour over sauce. Cover and cook in oven for 45 minutes at 350°F., Gas mark 4. Remove bay leaf before serving. If liked sprinkle with chopped parsley.

Noodles

12 oz. noodles
1–2 oz. butter

Cook noodles in plenty of boiling salted water according to directions on the packet, stirring occasionally. Drain well, melt butter in the saucepan and replace noodles. Stir lightly to coat with butter. Serve either in a heated dish or round the liver and kidney casserole.

Courgettes

1 lb. courgettes
salt; pepper
1–2 oz. butter

Wash the courgettes, trim ends, but leave unpeeled. Cut into ½ inch slanting slices. Melt butter, add courgettes, season and cook gently for 15–20 minutes. Shake the pan from time to time to prevent sticking: when nearly tender, remove the lid and increase heat slightly, to evaporate excess liquid. Serve in a hot dish.

Flan panachie

choux pastry using 4 oz. self-raising flour etc., see page 18

Almond pastry:
2 oz. ground almonds
4 oz. plain flour
1 oz. caster sugar
1 egg yolk
about 1 tablespoonful water

Filling:
2 oranges, peeled and broken into segments
a few white grapes, halved and de-seeded

Glaze:
2 tablespoonfuls apricot jam

To decorate:
1 oz. flaked almonds, browned in the oven
¼ pint double cream

Make almond pastry by mixing almonds and flour and proceeding as for flan pastry, see page 16. Roll out and line an 8-inch flan ring placed on a baking tray.
Place choux pastry in a piping bag fitted with a ½-inch plain pipe. Pipe mixture round the edge of the pastry and across the centre twice, at right angles, to divide the flan into 4. Pipe a small ball of mixture separately on to the baking tray. Bake flan for 30 minutes at 375°F., Gas mark 5. Cool on a wire tray then place on a serving dish. Heat jam and sieve it to make a glaze. Arrange oranges in 2 quarters of the flan and grapes in remaining quarters. Brush fruit and choux pastry with the glaze and use it to stick the choux ball in centre of flan. Sprinkle border with almonds and serve with whipped cream.

The flan may be made in the morning and filled and decorated whilst the main dish is in the oven.

Coffee, see page 114.

Mushroom vol-au-vents
Sweet and sour pork with rice
Mandarin gâteau
Coffee

Mushroom vol-au-vents

7½–8 oz. puff pastry
1 x 7½-oz. can creamed mushrooms, heated
a little beaten egg

If using frozen pastry allow to thaw for 1½–2 hours. Roll out pastry and cut 4 rounds using a 3-inch plain scone cutter. With a small (1-inch) cutter or apple corer press halfway through the pastry in the centre of each round. Brush with beaten egg. Roll out pastry trimmings and cut out 4 lids using the small cutter. Place pastry and lids on a wetted baking tray and bake for 15 minutes at 425°F., Gas mark 7, removing the lids when browned. With the handle of a teaspoon remove centre of each vol-au-vent, replace in the oven for 3 minutes to dry out the centre.
Fill with the creamed mushrooms, cover with the lids and keep hot until required.
Serve garnished with a sprig of parsley.

Vol-au-vent cases may be made the day before. Store the cooled cases overnight in an airtight tin or wrap them in aluminium foil. Before spooning in the mushroom filling place the cases on a baking tray and reheat them in a moderate oven.

Sweet and sour pork

1–1½ lb. lean blade of pork, cubed
2 onions, peeled and sliced
1 green pepper, cored and roughly chopped
1 oz. butter
1 oz. plain flour
¾ pint chicken stock
1 x 15-oz. can pineapple tidbits
2 tablespoonfuls malt vinegar
2 tablespoonfuls tomato ketchup
1 tablespoonful Worcestershire sauce
1 tablespoonful brown sugar
4 oz. mushrooms, quartered
salt
pepper
a few drops soy sauce

Lightly brown pork, onions and pepper in the melted butter. Stir in flour and cook for 1 minute. Gradually blend in stock, bring to the boil, stirring well. Add pineapple and juice with all other ingredients, including salt and pepper to taste. Stir well. Cover and simmer for about 1½ hours or until pork is tender.

Boiled rice

8 oz. long grain rice
4 teaspoonfuls salt

Fill a large saucepan two-thirds full of boiling water. Wash rice, add it to the boiling salted water and boil steadily according to the directions on the packet or until tender, stirring occasionally. Drain rice thoroughly, spread out on a shallow ovenproof dish and put into a warm oven. Cover with greased paper and stir once or twice. When pork is cooked arrange rice around the edge of a serving dish and pour the sweet and sour pork in the centre.

Mandarin gâteau

24 sponge finger biscuits
2 tablespoonfuls sherry
4 tablespoonfuls milk
$\frac{1}{4}$ pint double cream
2 teaspoonfuls coffee essence
2 teaspoonfuls caster sugar
1 oz. walnuts, chopped
1 x 11-oz. can mandarin oranges, drained

Dip 8 sponge fingers in sherry and milk and place close together on a flat serving dish. Whip cream, fold in coffee essence, sugar and walnuts. Spread a third of the cream mixture on top of the biscuits. Repeat the process twice more to make 2 more layers, finishing with the cream. Decorate with mandarin oranges. Serve chilled.

The gâteau may be made the night before and kept in the refrigerator. Take it out of the refrigerator about 30 minutes before the meal.

Coffee, see page 114.

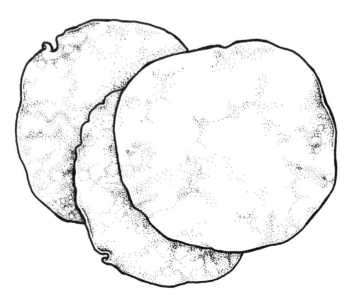

Menus for 6 people

Lamb curry with rice and accompaniments
Compote of melon and black grapes
Coffee

Lamb curry

2 lb. lean shoulder of lamb, cubed
2 onions, peeled and chopped
2 oz. butter
2 tablespoonfuls oil
4 tablespoonfuls curry powder or more according to taste
2 tablespoonfuls plain flour
$\frac{1}{2}$ teaspoonful ground ginger
1 pint beef stock or stock cube and water
1 tablespoonful mango chutney
1 teaspoonful black treacle
grated rind and juice 1 lemon
1 small cooking apple, peeled, cored and chopped
2 oz. sultanas
salt; pepper
2 cloves garlic, peeled and crushed (optional)

Lightly brown lamb and onion in the heated butter and oil. Stir in curry powder, flour and ginger and cook for 1 minute. Gradually blend in stock, bring to the boil stirring all the time. Add all remaining ingredients, cover and simmer for $1-1\frac{1}{2}$ hours until lamb is tender. Serve with boiled rice and accompaniments.

May be made the day before and reheated but take care not to overcook the meat.

Boiled rice

12 oz. long grain rice
6 teaspoonfuls salt

Prepare following directions opposite.

Some accompaniments for curry
Poppadums—heat according to instructions.
Mango or other chutney.
Salted almonds—fry shelled almonds in oil, drain and sprinkle with salt. Cucumber, sliced or diced, coated in natural yogurt and sprinkled with chopped chives. Sliced tomatoes in French dressing, see page 103. Sliced bananas sprinkled with lemon juice to prevent discolouration.
Drained pineapple cubes.
Thinly sliced onion rings.

Paella, page 109

Compote of melon and black grapes

2 oz. sugar
¼ pint water
1 melon
6 oz. black grapes, halved and de-pipped
a few fresh mint leaves

Dissolve sugar in the water, boil 2 minutes and cool. Remove the rind from the melon, cut in half and remove seeds. Either cut into balls with a small scoop or cut into cubes. Mix with the grapes. Pour the syrup over the fruit and coat well. Serve in 6 individual dishes and garnish with mint leaves.

May be prepared the night before or in the morning and stored in a covered container in the refrigerator. Serve in individual dishes and garnish when required.

Coffee, see page 114.

Tuna and shrimp cocktail
Steak, kidney and mushroom pie
New potatoes and
Brussels sprouts
Ginger ice cream
Coffee

Tuna and shrimp cocktail

½ lettuce, washed, dried and shredded
1 x 7-oz. can tuna fish, drained and flaked
1 x 5¼-oz. can shrimps, drained

Sauce:
5 tablespoonfuls mayonnaise
1 tablespoonful tomato ketchup
1 teaspoonful Worcestershire sauce
few drops Tabasco sauce
salt
cayenne pepper

To serve:
1 lemon, cut into wedges
brown bread, buttered

Blend together sauce ingredients. Place shredded lettuce on the base of 6 glasses. Mix tuna fish and shrimps, pile on top of lettuce and spoon sauce over fish mixture. Serve with lemon wedges and brown bread and butter.

Sauce may be made the day before, covered and stored in the refrigerator or a cold place. Lettuce may be washed and dried lightly in the morning and stored in a plastic bag.

Steak, kidney and mushroom pie

flaky or rough puff pastry using 8 oz. flour etc., see pages 16 and 18

1¼–1½ lb. chuck steak
4 lambs' kidneys
1 onion, peeled and chopped
1 oz. dripping or 2 tablespoonfuls oil
1 oz. plain flour
½ pint inexpensive red wine
½ pint stock or water
6 oz. button mushrooms, washed
salt; pepper

Trim meat, remove fat and cube. Wash and skin the kidneys, remove core and dice. Brown meat, kidney and onion in hot fat or oil. Stir in flour and cook for 1 minute. Gradually blend in wine and stock, bring to the boil stirring all the time. Add mushrooms and season to taste, cover and simmer 1¼ hours until meat is just tender. Pour into a pie dish and cool. Roll out pastry and place over pie dish, decorate, see page 31, and brush with beaten egg. Bake at 425°F., Gas mark 7 for 40 minutes, covering with greaseproof paper after 20 minutes.

Meat may be cooked the day before. Pastry may be made, wrapped well and stored overnight in the refrigerator.
If liked oysters can be added to the above pie. Halve 6 oysters and put them into the pie dish with the cooked meat.
Stand the pie dish on a baking tray to make it easier to remove the dish from the oven.

New potatoes

1½–2 lb. new potatoes
2 teaspoonfuls salt
a sprig mint
knob butter

Scrape potatoes, cover with boiling water, add salt and mint, simmer until tender (about 10–15 minutes). Drain, toss in a little butter and keep hot until required.

Brussels sprouts

2–2½ lb. sprouts
2 teaspoonfuls salt
½–1 oz. butter

Prepare sprouts, cook in boiling salted water until tender (about 10–15 minutes). Drain, toss in a little butter and serve in a hot dish.

Ginger ice cream

4 egg whites
4 tablespoonfuls icing sugar, sieved
½ pint double cream
3 pieces stem ginger, chopped
2 teaspoonfuls ginger syrup

Whisk egg whites until stiff and standing in peaks, gradually whisk in icing sugar. Whip cream until fairly stiff and fold into egg white and sugar mixture. Add ginger and syrup and fold in gently. Transfer mixture into a strong plastic container or ice tray (without divisions), cover and freeze.

Ice cream may be made ahead and frozen in the ice-making compartment of the refrigerator or in the freezer. If stored in freezer, transfer to the ice-making compartment of the refrigerator the day before the party.

Coffee, see page 114.

Cheesy eggs
Paella with celery and lettuce salad
Orange profiteroles
Coffee

Cheesy eggs

6 eggs, hardboiled
2 x 3-oz. packets cream cheese
salt; a little cayenne pepper
12 x 2¼-inch rounds brown bread, buttered
3 tomatoes, sliced

To garnish:
a little chopped parsley

Cut eggs in half, lengthways. Remove yolks and beat together with the cream cheese and seasonings. Transfer mixture to a forcing bag fitted with a large star pipe and pipe mixture into egg white cases, or fill using a teaspoon. Place a slice of tomato on each round of buttered bread, put the stuffed eggs on top and decorate with chopped parsley.

Paella

4 lb. roasting chicken, jointed
2 tablespoonfuls oil
2 oz. butter
2 onions, peeled and chopped
2 cloves garlic, peeled and crushed
6 oz. long grain rice
1 pint chicken stock
pinch saffron (optional)
1 red pepper, cored and chopped
salt; pepper
4 oz. runner beans, cooked
3 tomatoes, skinned, de-seeded and chopped
4 oz. prawns or scampi (other shellfish may also be added)

Brown chicken joints in the heated oil and butter. Remove, draining well and place in a casserole. Add onions and garlic to the fat. Cook until soft. Stir in the rice and cook for one minute. Add chicken stock, saffron and red pepper, bring to the boil, stirring well. Season with salt and pepper. Pour over the chicken and cook in oven at 375°F., Gas mark 5 for 35 minutes. Stir in the beans, tomatoes and prawns and continue cooking for a further 10 minutes. Serve piled up on a hot dish. Garnish with a few whole prawns.

Celery and lettuce salad

1 large lettuce
1 small head celery
double quantity French dressing, see page 103

Wash lettuce and dry in a cloth. Separate stalks of celery, clean thoroughly and dry. Shred lettuce and chop celery. Mix together in a salad bowl, toss salad in French dressing just before serving.

Lettuce and celery may be prepared the day before and stored in plastic bags in the refrigerator or a cold place until required.
French dressing may also be prepared ahead and stored in a cool place in a screw top jar or other suitable container.

Orange profiteroles

choux pastry using 4 oz. self-raising flour etc., see page 18

½ pint double cream
grated rind 1 orange

Orange glacé icing:
6 oz. icing sugar, sieved
orange juice

Pipe 18 balls of choux pastry on to a greased baking tray and bake as directed.
Split open while still hot and scoop out any soft centre, cool the choux balls on a wire tray. Whip the cream and fold in the grated orange rind. Fill the choux balls with the cream. Make the icing as directed on page 51, using enough orange juice to mix to a coating consistency. Coat the profiteroles and leave in a cold place to set.

The profiterole cases may be made a day ahead and stored in an airtight tin. If made in advance, re-crisp in a moderate oven, 350°F., Gas mark 4, for a few minutes and cool before filling and icing when required.

Coffee, see page 114.

Prawns with garlic mayonnaise
Cider-baked gammon with baked potatoes and broad beans
Apricot gâteau
Coffee

Prawns with garlic mayonnaise

lettuce leaves
12 oz. prawns (if frozen, allow to thaw)

To serve:
6 slices lemon
brown bread, buttered

Mayonnaise:
2 egg yolks
2 teaspoonfuls sugar
4 teaspoonfuls plain flour
pinch dry mustard
salt; pepper
1 oz. butter, melted
7 fl. oz. milk
3 fl. oz. wine or cider vinegar
2 cloves garlic, peeled and crushed

To make mayonnaise: blend together the egg yolks, sugar, flour, seasonings and melted butter, stir in the milk and transfer to a double saucepan (or use a basin over a pan of water). Blend in the vinegar and garlic and cook, stirring frequently for about 10 minutes until thick enough to coat the back of the spoon. Allow to cool, placing a piece of wet grease-proof paper over the surface to prevent a skin forming. Arrange lettuce leaves on 6 individual plates, pile prawns on top and coat with the mayonnaise.

Garlic mayonnaise may be made the day before, covered tightly and left overnight in the refrigerator or a cold place.

Cider-baked gammon

3½–4 lb. joint corner or middle gammon, soaked for a few hours or overnight in cold water
a few whole cloves
2 oz. soft brown sugar
1 teaspoonful made mustard
grated rind and juice 1 orange
⅛ pint cider
salt; pepper

Dry gammon and remove skin with a sharp knife. Score fat in a diamond pattern and stud with cloves. Place gammon on a large piece of foil in a roasting tin, draw up the sides of the foil. Mix together the brown sugar, mustard, orange rind and juice, cider and seasonings and pour over the joint. Wrap loosely in foil. Bake for 1 hour at 425°F., Gas mark 7, reduce heat to 400°F., Gas mark 6 and bake for a further 45 minutes–1 hour, until tender. Serve hot with cider sauce.

Baked potatoes

9 medium-sized potatoes, scrubbed and pricked

Place on a baking tray. Cook below the gammon until tender (about 1 hour). Serve with butter.

Broad beans

3–4 lb. fresh beans or **2 x 8-oz.** packets frozen beans

Shell beans and cook in boiling salted water for 15–20 minutes until tender or cook frozen beans as directed. Drain and toss lightly in butter.

Apricot gâteau

1 x 15-oz. can apricot halves, drained, reserving juice
2 sponge cakes, see page 48, baked in 2 x 7-inch tins for 12–15 minutes
¼ pint double cream, whipped

To decorate:
2–3 oz. walnuts, finely chopped
apricot glaze, see page 105
angelica, cut into 'leaves'

Spoon most of the apricot juice over the cakes and allow to soak for 5–10 minutes. Chop a few apricot halves roughly, stir into the whipped cream and use to sandwich the 2 cakes together. Brush sides of the gâteau with apricot glaze and press on the walnuts. Arrange apricot halves on top of cake. Brush glaze over the apricots and decorate with angelica 'leaves'.

Cakes may be made the day before, filled and decorated in the morning and stored in the refrigerator or in a cold place. Leave at room temperature for about 30 minutes before serving.

Coffee, see page 114.

Buffet party menus for 12 people

Creamed carrot soup
Pork paprika with buttered noodles and tossed green salad
Mandarin cloud
Coffee

Creamed carrot soup

3 lb. carrots, peeled and sliced
3 onions, peeled and sliced
2½ pints chicken stock or stock cubes and water
¾ pint single cream
salt; pepper

Simmer carrots and onions in stock until tender (about 30 minutes). Sieve or liquidise. Return to the saucepan, stir in the cream. When required, reheat (but do not boil) and check seasoning. Serve in warmed soup bowls or mugs, adding a few croûtons, see below, to each.

To make croûtons: allow half a large slice of bread per person. Remove crusts and cut bread into small dice. Heat a mixture of butter and oil in a frying pan and cook the croûtons turning them frequently until golden brown on all sides. Drain on kitchen paper and keep hot until required.

Soup may be prepared the day before or in the morning and kept, covered, in the refrigerator.

Pork paprika

1 lb. onions, peeled and chopped
4 tablespoonfuls oil
4½ lb. lean pork, in bite-sized pieces
2 oz. flour, plain or self-raising
6 tablespoonfuls tomato purée
6 tablespoonfuls paprika pepper
2 teaspoonfuls dried mixed herbs
2½ pints chicken stock or stock cubes and water
salt
1 lb. button mushrooms, washed

Fry the onions gently in the oil for 5 minutes, without browning. Add pork, fry for a further 5 minutes then stir in the flour, tomato purée, paprika pepper and herbs. Blend in the stock, bring to the boil and simmer for 1½–2 hours until the pork is tender; check seasoning. Add the mushrooms to the pork just before serving, reheat gently until boiling and simmer for 10–15 minutes. Serve with buttered noodles.

May be made on the morning of the party, reserving the mushrooms to add as directed before serving.

Buttered noodles, see page 104. Allow 3 oz. noodles per head.

Tossed green salad

4 lettuces
2 bunches watercress
2 green peppers, cored, halved and sliced
1 cucumber, sliced

French dressing:
$\frac{1}{2}$ pint olive oil
6−8 tablespoonfuls wine or cider vinegar
$\frac{1}{2}$ teaspoonful salt
$\frac{1}{2}$ teaspoonful sugar
pepper
1 teaspoonful made mustard

Wash the lettuce and watercress: store in polythene bags until required. Mix all French dressing ingredients in a screw top jar. When required arrange salad ingredients in large dishes. Shake dressing well and serve separately.

Mandarin cloud

3 x 11-oz. cans mandarin oranges
6 oz. sugar
$\frac{3}{4}$ pint water
1$\frac{1}{2}$ oz. gelatine
$\frac{1}{2}$ pint sherry
finely grated rind 2 oranges
9 egg whites

Drain mandarins, reserving syrup, and cut each into 2 or 3 pieces. Dissolve sugar in the water and bring to the boil. Simmer for 5 minutes. Dissolve gelatine in a little water and add to the sugar syrup, with the sherry, orange rind and mandarin syrup. When on the point of setting, fold in the stiffly beaten egg whites and beat until the mixture is snowy. Fold in the mandarins and divide between 12 individual dishes.

May be prepared on the morning of the party and kept in a cold place.

Coffee, see page 114.

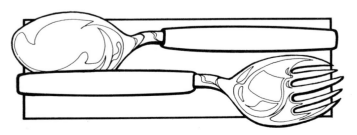

Salmon and cucumber mousse
Lamb with honey mustard sauce
Baked potatoes
Mocha whip
Coffee

Salmon and cucumber mousse

2 x 7-oz. cans salmon
1 cucumber
1 oz. gelatine
3 tablespoonfuls mayonnaise, see page 25
$\frac{1}{2}$ pint double cream
salt; pepper

To serve:
watercress
cucumber slices

Drain the salmon, remove the skin and large bones, mash smoothly. Peel cucumber, discard seeds and chop the flesh finely. Dissolve gelatine in 2 tablespoonfuls water. Mix together the salmon, mayonnaise, cucumber and gelatine, season to taste. Whip the cream until soft peaks form; fold into salmon mixture. Turn the mixture into a dish, smooth level and cover with foil. To serve, place a few sprigs of watercress or a few slices of cucumber on small plates and allow about 1 tablespoonful of mousse per person.

This may be prepared the day before.

Lamb with honey mustard sauce

3 lb. leg lamb, weighed after boning
2 onions, peeled and grated
1 tablespoonful Worcestershire sauce
salt; black pepper
1 egg beaten

Sauce:
4 tablespoonfuls made mustard
4 tablespoonfuls clear honey
4 tablespoonfuls soft brown sugar
2$\frac{1}{2}$ fl. oz. stock

Mince lamb finely, mix with the other ingredients. Make into about 48 small balls. Mix together the ingredients for the sauce. Just before required, fry the meat balls in shallow oil for about 10 minutes, shaking the pan occasionally to make sure they are cooked on all sides. Drain well and place in warmed dish. Heat the sauce ingredients and serve separately.

Baked potatoes, see page 111. Allow 2 medium-sized potatoes per head.

Mocha whip

8 oz. plain chocolate
3 oz. butter
2 tablespoonfuls instant coffee
2–3 tablespoonfuls brandy, rum or sherry
8 eggs, separated
1 pint single cream

Melt the chocolate in a basin over hot water, remove from heat. Stir in the butter, coffee powder, brandy, rum or sherry and egg yolks. Whisk the eggs whites until stiff and fold into the mixture. Divide between 12 individual dishes and allow to set. Just before serving, pour a little single cream on each mousse so that it forms a thin layer.

The mousse may be made the day before it is required.

Coffee, see page 114.

Drinks

The following notes will help you choose and order drinks for all occasions. The quantities given are only a rough guide (drinking capacities vary enormously), but if in doubt, always err on the generous side. Some large wine firms will supply drink in bulk on a sale or return basis. If money is tight, it is well worth taking the trouble to search out one of these rather than run the risk of running out.
Some off-licences will loan glasses free of charge if you purchase the drinks from them.

Spirits
1 bottle of whisky or gin serves about 20 people with mineral or soda water.

Sherry
Calculate somewhere between 10–12 glasses a bottle unless the glasses are very small. If sherry is served on its own, offer at least 2 types, preferably dry and medium dry. A sweet sherry may also be included.

Vermouth
This may be drunk on its own with a slice of lemon and ice, or with gin as a cocktail. Either way calculate about 10–12 glasses from a bottle. You have a choice of Bianco (sweet white), Italian (sweet red) or French (dry white).

Wine
Many people prefer a glass of wine to spirits or sherry. The standard British bottle gives 5–6 glasses on average. Serve a choice of white, slightly chilled, or red. Most red wine is best served at room temperature. For a wine party, litre bottles, half-gallon or gallon jars are available in the less expensive price range. Allow about 3 glasses per head.

Champagne
Serving champagne alone at a party may seem extravagant but, if a non-vintage champagne is chosen, it will cost no more than the usual selection of spirits and is infinitely less trouble! Allow a third to half a bottle per head. 1 bottle gives 6–8 glasses.

Beer
For parties buy 4- or 7-pint cans rather than the usual individual cans or bottles.
If the party is to be a large one, it may be worth considering buying a small barrel.

Soft drinks
Always have a supply of tomato juice, fruit juices or squash at hand. Not only do many people prefer non-alcoholic beverages, but talking is thirsty work and spirits and wines are not very thirst-quenching. Squash or cordial can be diluted and served with lemon or orange slices and ice.

Wine and cider cups
These are always popular and are ideal for summer parties.

White wine cup

makes 2½ pints:
1 bottle dry or medium white wine
2 tablespoonfuls Grand Marnier or brandy
2 x 11½-fl. oz. bottles soda water
1 lemon, thinly sliced
crushed ice

Mix wine, Grand Marnier and soda in a jug or bowl and chill. Serve with lemon slices and crushed ice.

Cider cup

makes just over 3 pints:
1 quart sweet or dry cider
1 pint soda water
1 tablespoonful brandy
few strips cucumber rind
few strips lemon rind
1 tablespoonful lemon juice for sweet cider or 1 tablespoonful orange juice for dry cider
2 teaspoonfuls caster sugar

Chill bottles of cider and soda water. Put brandy, cucumber, lemon rind, fruit juice and sugar in a large jug and mix all ingredients just before serving.

Sangria

makes 2½ pints:
1 bottle Spanish or Portugese red wine
1 large bottle lemonade
slice lemon
1 liqueur glass brandy
slices apple and orange
caster sugar

Chill equal quantities of wine and lemonade. Just before serving mix in all remaining ingredients, adding a little sugar to taste but avoid making the drink sweet.

Summer punch (non-alcoholic)

makes about 5 pints:
1 x 20-fl. oz. can grapefruit juice, chilled
1 x 20-fl. oz. can orange juice, chilled
½ pint cold tea, strained
2 pints cold water or soda water
½ bottle ginger cordial
4 oz. sugar
few sprigs mint and thinly sliced cucumber

Put all ingredients in a large bowl or jug, stir well to dissolve the sugar. Serve garnished with mint leaves and cucumber and add a few lumps of ice.

Mulled wine

makes about 1½ pints:
1 bottle dry red wine
4 oz. caster sugar
juice 1 lemon
juice 1 orange
½ teaspoonful ground cinnamon
6 cloves

Place all ingredients in a saucepan and heat gently, stirring to dissolve the sugar. When hot (do not allow the wine to boil), strain into warmed glasses.

Ice

This is a must for all parties: even if your drinks start in the refrigerator (and you'll be very lucky if there's room in it for all of them), they very soon warm up to room temperature, and as the room temperature warms up as fast as the party does, it won't be long before you're offering long tepid drinks instead of long cool ones. So you need ice, and you need a lot of it. The place to go for this is your local fishmonger: give him plenty of warning, tell him the size and date of your party and, with luck, he will do the rest—and charge a very reasonable price for it. The ice should be delivered—or collected—on the day of the party so that storage problems are only temporary and melting reduced to a minimum. Put it in a tin or plastic bath and leave in a cool place until needed.

Coffee

When making coffee in large quantities you will find it easier to use instant rather than ground. A 2-oz. jar or can with 8 pints of water will make about 24—25 cups with hot milk or cream and 1½ lb. of brown or coffee sugar. If you are using ground coffee, allow 1 oz. per person. Warm an earthenware jug and place the ground coffee in it. Pour on boiling water, allowing ½ pint per 1 oz. coffee. Leave to infuse for 5 minutes, strain and pour into a warmed coffee pot. This may be done before the coffee is needed: stand the coffee pot in a pan of hot water until required.

Tea

As the ratio of tea to water varies tremendously according to individual taste and according to the vessel it's made in, we can only give a rough middle-of-the-road guide to make a medium-strong cuppa. Allow 3 oz. tea per 8 pints boiling water, leave 3—5 minutes to infuse. This will make about 24—25 cups. The easiest way out of the dilemma of providing **everyone** with a cup of tea to their liking is to use tea bags: one per cup and leave the drinker to make his tea as weak or strong as he likes.

Children's party drinks

Orange honey drink

1 x 16-oz. can orange juice
1 bottle soda water
juice 6 oranges or another **16-oz.** can orange juice
1 tablespoonful clear honey

Mix together and chill before serving.

Orange honey drink; blackcurrant and lemon refresher, chocolate, coffee, blackcurrant and orange milk shakes, and hot chocolate peppermint drink, page 116

Blackcurrant and lemon refresher

$\frac{1}{4}$ pint lemon squash
$\frac{1}{4}$ pint blackcurrant juice
$1\frac{1}{2}$ pints cold water

Mix together and chill before serving.

Frosted glasses

Frosted glasses are attractive for serving cold drinks: moisten the rim of the glass with water and dip in caster or coffee sugar. Allow to dry overnight. Decorate edge of glass with an orange or lemon slice cut through half-way and placed over the edge of the glass.

Milk shakes

These have the virtue of being both popular with and good for children. To make one, simply whisk together milk and flavouring or place in a blender for a few seconds. Allow 1 pint of milk for 3 children.

Chocolate

1 pint milk
$\frac{1}{2}$ small block chocolate ice cream

Orange

1 pint milk
2 tablespoonfuls concentrated frozen orange juice

Blackcurrant

1 pint milk
2 tablespoonfuls blackcurrant cordial

Coffee

1 pint milk
2 tablespoonfuls coffee essence
sugar to taste

Peanut butter

1 pint milk
few drops vanilla essence
pinch cinnamon
2 tablespoonfuls peanut butter

Hot chocolate peppermint drink

1 pint milk
2 oz. chocolate peppermint creams or **1 x 2-oz.** chocolate bar

Heat gently until chocolate melts.

Fruit punch

2 pints non-alcoholic cider
2 x 18-oz. cans grapefruit juice
2 x 18-oz. cans pineapple juice
$\frac{1}{4}$ pint orange squash
soda water
2 red apples
few black and green grapes

Mix together the liquid ingredients in a large bowl, adding soda water to taste. Wash the apples, cut into four, remove core and slice thinly. Wash and halve grapes, removing the pips. Float the fruit on top of the punch, adding a few ice cubes if desired.

Creamy coke

Place a scoop of ice cream in tall glasses and fill up with Coca Cola. Top with a spoonful of lightly whipped cream.

Strawberry cream

4 oz. strawberries
1 tablespoonful icing sugar
1 pint milk
1 small block vanilla ice cream

Crush the strawberries and mix with the icing sugar. Add the milk and ice cream and whisk well or mix all ingredients in an electric blender.

Quick meals and snacks

It may be unjust to call it the twentieth century's contribution to the table, but the quick snack in all its guises—from the pre-packed meal trays served on aeroplanes and the busy secretary's bite of cheese and celery at lunch to the working mother's family supper in five minutes—is obviously here to stay. If money's no problem, nor is the snack—there's caviar, smoked salmon, minute steaks and boeuf stroganoff for a start—but if it is (and that applies to most of us) make the most of nature's perfect pre-packed standby, the egg: it's as valuable, versatile and quick to prepare as any food we have. And don't despise man's own contribution in this direction—baked beans. Just because the meal takes five minutes to buy and as many minutes to prepare there's no need for it to be boring, however slim your resources: we've written this section to prove it. With a few simple ingredients (most of them from the store cupboard) and a few precious minutes you'll find you can cook a snack or meal fit to grace any table.

Happy eating . . .

Chinese corn soup

serves 4:
1 x 7-oz. can sweetcorn niblets
1½ pints chicken stock or water and stock cubes
salt; pepper
2 eggs, beaten

Empty sweetcorn into a saucepan, add stock and seasoning. Bring to the boil, stir in the beaten eggs and cook gently for one minute. Serve immediately.

Mushroom and chicken soup

serves 4:
1 x 7½-oz. can creamed mushrooms
1 pint milk
1 x 3-oz. jar chicken in jelly, diced, or 1 x 5-oz. can ham and chicken roll, diced
salt; pepper

Combine all ingredients and heat thoroughly. Serve hot with toast or croûtons, see page 111.

Summer tomato soup

Wash an orange, grate the rind using the finest part of the grater. Squeeze out the juice. Add rind and juice of the orange to the contents of a 15¼-oz. can tomato soup and heat. Serve garnished with parsley.

Pea and bacon soup

serves 4:
1 x 15½-oz. can processed peas
½ pint milk
¼ pint water
4 rashers streaky bacon, de-rinded and chopped, fried until crisp
salt
pepper

Sieve or liquidise peas. Add remaining ingredients and heat through. Serve hot with toast or croûtons, see page 111.

Frankfurt bean soup

serves 4:
1 x 16-oz. can baked beans
½ pint milk
¼ pint water
4 frankfurter sausages, sliced, or small can cocktail sausages, drained
salt; pepper

Sieve or liquidise beans. Add remaining ingredients and heat through. Serve hot with toast or croûtons, see page 111.

Beef goulash soup

serves 4:
1 x 7½-oz. can minced beef with onion
2 tablespoonfuls tomato purée
4 teaspoonfuls paprika pepper
salt
1½ pints beef stock

Combine beef, tomato purée, paprika and salt in a saucepan. Add stock, bring to the boil, stirring well. Cover and simmer for 5–8 minutes. Serve hot with toast.

Onion and pasta soup

serves 4:
1 medium onion, peeled and chopped
1 oz. butter
1½ pints beef stock
1 oz. pasta shapes
salt; pepper

Fry onion in melted butter until golden. Add beef stock, pasta and seasoning, bring to the boil. Cover and simmer for 15 minutes. Serve hot with French bread.

Beef 'n' bean hash

Pizza special

serves 4–6:
Scone base:
6 oz. self-raising flour
1 oz. butter or margarine
3 oz. cheese, grated
salt
cayenne pepper
pinch dry mustard
1 egg
2 tablespoonfuls milk

Topping:
4 oz. salami or garlic sausage, sliced and de-rinded
4 slices processed cheddar cheese
4 large tomatoes, sliced
1 small can anchovies, drained
a few stuffed olives, sliced

Prepare scone base by the rubbing-in method, see page 19, knead lightly and roll out into an 8-inch round. Place on a lightly greased baking tray. Arrange salami overlapping on scone base, cover with cheese, top with tomatoes. Halve anchovies lengthways, place in a criss-cross design on top. Bake for 25 minutes at 400°F., Gas mark 6. Decorate with sliced olives. Serve hot.

Curried potato soup

serves 4:
1 x 2½-oz. packet instant potato mix
2 tablespoonfuls curry powder
1 pint boiling water
½ pint milk
salt; pepper
1 oz. sultanas

Mix together potato and curry powder. Pour over 1 pint boiling water, stirring well. Stir in milk, seasoning and sultanas, bring to the boil. Cover and simmer for 5 minutes. Serve hot with toast.

Beef 'n' bean hash

serves 4:
1 onion, peeled and sliced
2 tablespoonfuls oil
1 x 2½-oz. packet instant potato mix
1 x 7-oz. can corned beef, chopped
1 x 8-oz. can baked beans
salt; pepper

Fry onion in heated oil until soft. Prepare potato mix as directed on packet. Beat in the corned beef and beans, season with salt and pepper. Add hash mixture to onions and fry, turning frequently until crisp and golden (about 10 minutes). Serve hot sprinkled with parsley and if liked, a few fried onion rings.

Sausage and rice casserole

serves 4:
1 onion, peeled and sliced
1 lb. large pork sausages
1 tablespoonful oil
1 x 10¼-oz. can tomato soup + ½ can water
4 oz. long grain rice, cooked and drained

Brown onion and sausages in hot oil. Remove and place in a casserole. Combine soup, water and rice and pour over the sausages. Bake for 25 minutes at 400°F., Gas mark 6.

Sunshine snacks

serves 4:
4 slices cooked ham, cut into rounds
4 rounds toast or 4 crumpets, buttered
4 pineapple rings
4 teaspoonfuls chutney
4 oz. cheese, grated
parsley

Place rounds of ham on toast, top with pineapple rings and place a teaspoonful of chutney in each ring. Sprinkle with cheese and place under a hot grill until cheese melts and turns golden brown. Decorate with sprigs of parsley.

Tomato egg fluff

serves 4:
1 x 8-oz. can tomatoes
1 x 5-oz. packet instant potato mix
salt; pepper
4 eggs
2 oz. cheese, grated

Mix tomatoes with ¾ pint water and bring to the boil, add dry potato mix, beating thoroughly. Season with salt and pepper. Place potato into an ovenproof dish and make four hollows with a spoon. Break an egg into each hollow. Sprinkle with cheese and bake for 15–20 minutes at 375°F., Gas mark 5.

Curried scrambled eggs

serves 4:
1 onion, peeled and chopped
2 oz. butter
1 tablespoonful curry powder
1 tablespoonful milk
6 eggs, beaten
salt; pepper
2 tablespoonfuls mango chutney
4 slices toast, buttered

Fry onion in melted butter in a covered pan until soft (about 5 minutes); add curry powder, fry for 1 minute. Add milk to eggs, season with salt and pepper, mix in the chutney. Pour mixture on to onions and scramble, stirring constantly. Pile on to hot toast and serve immediately.

Pasta medley

1 small onion, chopped
1 oz. butter or margarine
1 oz. flour, plain or self-raising
1 pint milk
2 oz. cheese, grated
salt; pepper
1 x 7½-oz. can mushrooms, drained
4 oz. cooked ham, chopped
6 oz. macaroni or pasta shapes, cooked and drained
chopped parsley

Fry onion in melted fat in a covered pan until soft but not brown, add flour and cook for 1 minute. Gradually blend in the milk, bring to the boil, stirring well. Stir in the cheese, seasoning, mushrooms, ham and macaroni. Heat through for about 5 minutes. Serve hot, sprinkled with chopped parsley.

Italian spaghetti

serves 4:
1 x 8-oz. can tomatoes
¼ pint water
1 tablespoonful Worcestershire sauce
1 tablespoonful dried flaked onions
salt; pepper
1 x 7-oz. can luncheon meat, cut into thin strips
6 oz. spaghetti or long macaroni
2 oz. cheese, grated

Combine tomatoes, water, sauce, onions and seasoning, place in a pan, cover and simmer for 10 minutes. Stir in the luncheon meat and heat through.
Meanwhile cook spaghetti in boiling salted water until tender (about 10 minutes), drain, place in serving dish and pour over the sauce. Sprinkle with cheese and brown under the grill. If liked garnish with chopped parsley.

Savoury pilaff

serves 4:
1 onion, peeled and chopped
4 oz. streaky bacon, de-rinded and chopped
1 oz. butter or margarine
6 oz. long grain rice
1 pint chicken stock
pepper
1 tablespoonful dried parsley or mixed dried peppers
4 tomatoes, skinned, de-seeded and chopped

Fry onion and bacon in melted fat for 5 minutes. Stir in the rice and cook for one minute. Add stock, pepper and parsley and bring to the boil. Cover and simmer for 15 minutes, stirring occasionally. Stir in the tomatoes and cook for 5 minutes.

Liver and bacon parcels

serves 4:
4 slices lamb's liver, washed and dried
8 rashers lean bacon, de-rinded, chopped
2 onions, peeled and sliced
2 potatoes, peeled and thinly sliced
1 teaspoonful dried thyme
salt; pepper
8 tablespoonfuls stock or water

Place slices of liver on 4 separate pieces of buttered foil. Cover with layers of bacon, onion and potatoes. Sprinkle with thyme and seasoning; pour 2 tablespoonfuls stock on to each portion. Draw up the sides of the foil and make a loose 'parcel'. Place 'parcels' on a baking tray and bake for 45 minutes at 400°F., Gas mark 6.

Bacon and egg crumble

serves 4:
4 oz. streaky bacon, de-rinded and chopped
1 oz. butter or margarine
1 oz. flour, plain or self-raising
½ pint milk
6 tablespoonfuls canned sweetcorn niblets, drained
salt; pepper
4 hardboiled eggs, halved

Crumble:
1½ oz. soft white breadcrumbs
1 oz. butter

Fry bacon until crisp, add butter and allow to melt. Stir in the flour and cook for one minute. Gradually blend in the milk, bring to the boil, stirring all the time. Add sweetcorn and seasoning. Place eggs in an ovenproof dish, pour over the sauce mixture, sprinkle with breadcrumbs and dot with butter. Brown under the grill.

Sardine crumpets

serves 6:
1 can sardines, drained and mashed
2 tomatoes, skinned and chopped
6 crumpets, toasted and buttered
3 oz. cheese, grated
3 stuffed olives, sliced

Mix together sardines and tomatoes and spread over crumpets. Sprinkle with cheese, grill until golden brown. Decorate with sliced olives.

Salmon crisp

serves 4:
1 x 7½-oz. can salmon, drained
4 tablespoonfuls canned peas, drained
1 x 10¼-oz. can cream of mushroom soup

Topping:
½ **oz.** butter or margarine
1 oz. flour, plain of self-raising
1 small packet potato crisps, crushed

Flake salmon, removing skin and bones, combine with peas and soup and place in an ovenproof dish. Rub fat into flour and mix with the crisps. Sprinkle topping over salmon mixture and bake for 25–30 minutes at 375°F., Gas mark 5, until golden.

Chicken drumsticks

4 cooked chicken drumsticks

Spicy sauce:
2 tablespoonfuls mango chutney
2 tablespoonfuls tomato ketchup
2 tablespoonfuls fruit sauce
1 tablespoonful Worcestershire sauce
few drops soy and Tabasco sauce

Mix sauce ingredients together and serve with the chicken drumsticks.

Above: Swiss meringue, page 124
Above left: Salmon loaf
Below left: Beef and cheese cobbler

Salmon loaf

1 x 7½-oz. can salmon, drained and flaked
(removing skin and bones)
1 x 7½-oz. can potato salad
2 hardboiled eggs, chopped
4 oz. cucumber, chopped
1 tablespoonful chopped parsley
1 oz. soft white breadcrumbs
salt; pepper
lemon, green pepper and parsley to garnish

Mix all ingredients well. Transfer mixture to a 1-lb.
loaf tin, smooth level and chill.
To serve turn out on to a serving dish and surround
with a selection of salad vegetables. Garnish with a
twist of lemon and green pepper and a sprig of
parsley.

Beef and cheese cobbler

serves 4:
1 x 15½-oz. can minced beef with onion
1 x 8-oz. can tomatoes
½ teaspoonful mixed dried herbs
salt; pepper
cheese scone mixture using **8 oz.** flour etc., see
page 56
milk

Combine minced beef, tomatoes, herbs and seasoning in an ovenproof dish. Knead scone mixture lightly,
roll out to ½ inch thickness. Cut out rounds using
2-inch plain cutter. Arrange scones overlapping on
top of beef mixture. Brush with milk and bake for 25
minutes at 400°F., Gas mark 6, second shelf.

Apple cake

serves 6–8:
2 lb. cooking apples, peeled, cored and sliced
2 oz. dark soft brown sugar
a little water
4 oz. butter or margarine
8 oz. soft white breadcrumbs
1 teaspoonful ground cinnamon

Grease an 8-inch sandwich tin. Place apples and
sugar in a saucepan with water, cover and stew
until soft. Melt fat, stir in the breadcrumbs and cook
until golden, stirring well. Mix in the cinnamon.
Spread half the crumbs on the base of the tin. Cover
with apple mixture, spreading to the edges of the tin,
finish with a layer of crumbs. Bake for 25 minutes at
375°F., Gas mark 5. Serve cold from the tin with
cream or ice cream.

123

Golden gooseberry crumble

serves 4–6:
1 large can gooseberries
3 oz. raisins
8 oz. sponge cake, crumbled
3 oz. demerara sugar

Place fruit and raisins in an ovenproof dish. Mix together cake crumbs and sugar and sprinkle over the fruit. Bake 20–25 minutes at 400°F., Gas mark 6 until golden.
Serve hot or cold with custard or cream.

Strawberry treats

serves 4:
4 tablespoonfuls strawberry jam
4 slices buttered toast
1 egg white
2 oz. caster sugar

Spread jam on toast. Whisk egg white stiffly and gradually whisk in the sugar until 'peaky'. Spread meringue over jam and place under a low grill until golden (about 5 minutes). Serve at once.

Swiss meringue

serves 4:
4 x ½-inch thick slices Swiss roll
1 small can pineapple slices, drained, reserving juice

Meringue:
1 egg white
2 oz. caster sugar

To decorate:
2 glacé cherries, quartered
few angelica leaves

Place Swiss roll slices in individual ovenproof dishes and pour over the pineapple juice. Place a pineapple slice on top of each slice of Swiss roll. Whisk egg white stiffly and gradually whisk in the sugar until stiff and 'peaky'. Pile meringue over pineapple, place under a low grill and cook until golden brown (about 5 minutes). Decorate with cherries and angelica. Serve hot or cold.

Fruit meringue

serves 4:
2 eggs, separated
1 x 14½-oz. can fruit pie filling
4 oz. caster sugar

Mix egg yolks and pie filling and place in an oven-proof dish. Whisk egg whites stiffly and gradually whisk in the sugar a little at a time until stiff and 'peaky'. Pile meringue on top of fruit and fluff up with a fork. Bake for about 20 minutes at 350°F., Gas mark 4 until meringue is a pale golden colour. Serve hot or cold.

Pear sundae

4 oz. plain chocolate
½ **oz.** butter
1 teaspoonful instant coffee powder
1 tablespoonful boiling water
1 small block vanilla ice cream
1 x 16-oz. can pears

Melt the chocolate in a basin over hot water, add the butter and coffee dissolved in the boiling water, mix well. Divide ice cream between four individual dishes, top with drained pear halves. Spoon chocolate mixture over the top.

Quick fritters

1 egg
1 tablespoonful milk
4 slices white bread, each cut into two
1 oz. butter
1 tablespoonful oil
black cherry jam

Beat the egg and milk. Cut the crusts from the bread and dip the pieces in the egg and milk. Fry in hot butter and oil until pale golden brown. Drain on absorbent paper and serve with a spoonful of jam on each fritter.

Index

Aberdeen butteries 66
Almond:
    Almond jumbles 60
    Almond paste 52–3
    Almond pastry 105
    Almond slices 35
    Almond walnut loaf 96
    Cherry almond cake 47
    Cherry almond pancakes 42
    Salted almonds 69
Anchovies on toast 69
Apple:
    Apple cake 123
    Dutch apple pancakes 41
    Dutch apple tart 34
    Pork and apple pudding 32
    Toffee apples 94
    Waldorf salad 73
Apricot:
    Apricot crown gâteau 74
    Apricot gâteau 111
    Apricot jam sauce 37
    Golden apricot crumble 96
    Lamb and apricot pudding 32
Asparagus:
    Asparagus quiche 101
    Asparagus rolls 70
    Crab and asparagus flan 29

Bacon:
    To roast bacon 12
    Bacon and egg crumble 121
    Bacon and egg pie 29
    Bacon and egg sandwiches 88
    Bacon and pineapple flan 29
    Bacon roll 29
    Bacon sandwiches 88
    Liver and bacon parcels 121
Baked alaska 40
Bakewell tart 32
Banana butter sandwiches 88
Barbecue sauce 24
Barbecued beans 92
Batters 41. *See also* Pancakes
Beans:
    Barbecued beans 92
    Beef 'n' bean hash 119
    Broad beans 111
    Frankfurt bean soup 117
    Hawaiian beans 92
Béchamel sauce 24
Beef. *See also* Steak
    To roast beef 12
    Beef 'n' bean hash 119
    Beef and cheese cobbler 123
    Beef goulash soup 117
    Beef and tomato pudding 32
    Hamburgers with variations 90
Beer 113
Biscuits:
    Almond jumbles 60
    Butter fingers 58
    Cheese and olive biscuits 69
    Cheese straws 69
    Cheesy oat biscuits 82
    Chocolate chip cookies 62
    Chocolate crunchy biscuits 95
    Easter biscuits 62
    Empire biscuits 60
    Flapjacks 94
    Garibaldi biscuits 61
    Gingerbread men 59
    Gipsy creams 61

Grantham gingerbreads 58
Grasmere shortcake 61
Florentines 61
Hungarian chocolate biscuits 60
Melting moments 59
Party mice 96
Rich chocolate biscuits 62
Skye shortbread 58
Toffee bars 94
Blackcurrant and lemon refresher 116
Blackcurrant milk shake 116
Brack 63
Brandied coffee charlotte 74
Brandy butter 38
Bread (made with yeast). *See also* Teabreads
    Bread rolls 66
    Milk twist 64
    Simple currant bread 66
    White bread 64
Bridge rolls, filled 70
Brown sauce 22
Brussels sprouts 108
Buffet dishes 70, 72–7
Buffet meals 68–9
Bun loaf 63
Buns:
    Aberdeen butteries 66
    Chelsea buns 67
    Coffee cream buns 44, 84
    Cream buns 37
    Honey buns 44
    Hot cross buns 67
    Rum babas 67
Butter creams 50–1
Butter fingers 58
Butterflies 43

Cakes:
    To cover rich fruit cakes with almond
        paste and royal icing 51–5
    To line a cake tin 20
    To make by creaming method 19
    To make by melting method 19
    To make by one-stage method 20
    To make by rubbing-in method 19
    To make by whisking method 19
    To put things right in cake making 19
    Baking times for cakes 21
    Cake fillings and icings 50–5
Cakes, large:
    Apple cake 123
    Cherry almond cake 47
    Cherry cake 47
    Chocolate cake 47
    Chocolate log 50
    Chocolate sandwich 45
    Christmas cake 48
    Coconut sandwich 45
    Coffee walnut cake 47
    Cut and come again cake 46
    Date and walnut cake 46
    Dundee cake 47
    Frosted christening cake 85
    Fruit cake 46
    Genoese sponge 50
    Gingerbread 48
    Lardy cake 66
    Madeira cake 45
    Mandarin jelly cake 96
    Orange drizzle cake 95
    Orange sandwich 45
    Parkin 48
    Rich dark cake 48

Simnel cake 46
Sponge cake 48
Swiss roll 50
Victoria sandwich 45
Walnut sandwich 45
Wedding cake, two-tier 78
Wedding cake, three-tier 79
Cakes, small:
    Butterflies 43
    Chocolate cakes 43
    Chocolate peppermint bars 94
    Eccles cakes 35
    Fairy fruit cakes 42
    Ginger cakes 44
    Iced cherry cakes 42
    Iced honey cakes 43
    Iced pineapple cakes 42
    Queen cakes 42
    Raspberry buns 44
    Rock cakes 44
    Sponge drops 84
    Strawberry and grape rosettes 84
    Viennese rosettes 44
Caper sauce 24
Carrot:
    Cream of carrot soup 28
    Creamed carrot soup 111
Casserole:
    Orange duck casserole 103
    Sausage and rice casserole 120
Cauliflower:
    Cream of cauliflower soup 28
Celery:
    Celery and lettuce salad 109
    Cream of celery soup 28
Champagne 113
Cheese:
    Beef and cheese cobbler 123
    Cheese and ham dip 89
    Cheese and ham sandwiches 88
    Cheese nuts 83
    Cheese and olive biscuits 69
    Cheese and onion dip 88
    Cheese pastry 16
    Cheese and pickle sandwiches 88
    Cheese sauce 22
    Cheese scones 56
    Cheese and shrimp dip 89
    Cheese soufflé 25
    Cheese straws 69
    Cheese tartlets 28
    Cheese whirls 92
    Cheesy eggs 109
    Cheesy oat biscuits 82
    Cottage cornets 104
    Cream cheese horns 70
    Cream cheese and jam sandwiches 88
    Hot cheese dip 89
    Savoury cheese tartlets 89
    Shrimp and cheese flan 29
Chelsea buns 67
Cherry:
    Cherry almond cake 47
    Cherry almond pancakes 42
    Cherry cake 47
    Cherry scones 95
    Iced cherry cakes 42
Chicken:
    To roast chicken 12
    Chicken drumsticks 121
    Chicken liver pâté 72
    Chicken and orange sandwiches 88
    Chicken and pork pâté 73

Chicken and sweetcorn flan 29
Chicken and walnut tartlets 83
Curried chicken tartlets 72
Mushroom and chicken soup 117
Onion and chicken liver flan 29
Paella 109
Children's parties 88—97
Chinese corn soup 117
Chocolate:
Chocolate butter cream 50
Chocolate cake 47
Chocolate cakes 43
Chocolate chip cookies 62
Chocolate clusters 85
Chocolate crunchy biscuits 95
Chocolate éclairs 37
Chocolate fudge 97
Chocolate fudge icing 51
Chocolate fudge pudding 41
Chocolate glacé icing 51
Chocolate log 50
Chocolate milk shake 116
Chocolate peppermint bars 94
Chocolate pudding 37
Chocolate sandwich 45
Chocolate sauce 37
Chocolate soufflé 27
Hot chocolate peppermint drink 116
Hungarian chocolate biscuits 60
Mocha whip 113
Rich chocolate biscuits 62
Rich chocolate icing 51
Choux pastry 18
Christening cake 85
Christening parties 82—5
Christmas cake 48
Christmas pudding 38
Cider-baked gammon 110
Cider cup 113
Cinnamon crunch loaf 63
Cocktail snacks 69—70
Coconut sandwich 45
Coffee:
To make coffee 114
Brandied coffee charlotte 74
Coffee butter cream 50
Coffee cream buns 44, 84
Coffee glacé icing 51
Coffee meringues 84
Coffee milk shake 116
Coffee soufflé 27
Coffee walnut cake 47
Compote of melon and black grapes 108
Continental sandwiches 88
Corn-on-the-cob:
Chicken and sweetcorn flan 29
Chinese corn soup 117
Cottage cornets 104
Courgettes 105
Crab and asparagus flan 29
Crab and coleslaw salad 100
Cream buns 37
Cream caramels 76
Cream cheese horns 70
Cream cheese and jam sandwiches 88
Cream horns 35
Cream of vegetable soups 28
Creamed carrot soup 111
Creamy coke 116
Crispy peanut sandwiches 88
Crispy sandwiches 92
Crispy tartlets 89

Cucumber:
Cucumber soup 103
Salmon and cucumber mousse 112
Currant bread 66
Curried dishes:
Accompaniments for curry 106
Curried chicken tartlets 72
Curried potato soup 119
Curried scrambled eggs 120
Curry sauce 24
Lamb curry 106
Cut and come again cake 46

Date and walnut cake 46
Date and walnut loaf 62
Date and walnut scones 56
Desserts. *See also* Gâteaux, pies and tarts
Apple cake 123
Baked alaska 40
Brandied coffee charlotte 74
Compote of melon and black grapes 108
Cream caramels 76
Fresh fruit salad 103
Fruit meringue 124
Fruit salad 73
Ginger ice cream 109
Jelly fingers 93
Jelly oranges 93
Mandarin cloud 112
Mandarin jelly cake 96
Mocha whip 113
Orange profiteroles 110
Pear sundae 124
Pineapple nut slice 77
Plain and coffee meringues 84
Sherry trifle 74
Strawberry palmiers 101
Strawberry treats 124
Swiss meringue 124
Trifle-in-a-trifling 93
Yogurt jellies 95
Devils on horseback 84
Dips:
Cheese and onion dip 88
Cheese and ham dip 89
Cheese and shrimp dip 89
Hot cheese dip 89
Dropped scones 58
Duck:
Orange duck casserole 103
Dundee cake 47
Dutch apple pancakes 41
Dutch apple tart 34

Easter biscuits 62
Eccles cakes 35
Egg:
Bacon and egg crumble 121
Bacon and egg pie 29
Bacon and egg sandwiches 88
Cheesy eggs 109
Crispy tartlets 89
Curried scrambled eggs 120
Egg sauce 24
Stuffed eggs 83
Tomato egg fluff 120
Empire biscuits 60

Fairy fruit cakes 42
Fats, types of 13
Fish:
Amounts to buy per person 14
Fish soufflé 25

Mixed fish pâté 73
Smoked fish turnover 31
Flaky pastry 16
Flan pastry 16
Flans. See Tarts, tartlets and flans
Flapjacks 94
Florentines 61
Flours, types of 13; to store 13
Frangipane flan 76
French dressing 112
Fritters:
Fruit fritters 42
Quick fritters 124
Frosted christening cake 85
Frosted glasses 116
Fruit. *See also* Apple, apricot etc.
Fresh fruit salad 103
Fruit cake 46
Fruit crumble 41
Fruit fritters 42
Fruit meringue 124
Fruit pie 32
Fruit punch 116
Fruit salad 73
Fruit scones 56
Steamed fruit pudding 40
Fudge icing 51

Gammon:
Cider-baked gammon 110
Garibaldi biscuits 61
Garlic mayonnaise 110
Gâteaux:
Apricot crown gâteau 74
Apricot gâteau 111
Mandarin gâteau 106
Genoese sponge 50
Ginger cakes 44
Ginger ice cream 109
Ginger upsidedown pudding 39
Gingerbread 48
Gingerbread men 59
Gipsy creams 61
Girdle scones 56
Glacé icings 51
Gooseberry crumble 124
Grantham gingerbreads 58
Grasmere shortcake 61
Gravy for roast meat 24

Ham:
To roast ham 12
Ham and pineapple sandwiches 88
Ham soufflé 25
Hamburgers with variations 90
Hawaiian beans 92
Hollandaise sauce 24
Honey banana pancakes 42
Honey buns 44
Honey cakes, iced 43
Honey and nut fluff 104
Hot cross buns 67
Hungarian chocolate biscuits 60

Icings and fillings:
To decorate a cake 54
To ice a cake 54
To make and fill a paper icing bag 54
Almond paste 52—3
Butter creams 50—1
Fudge icing 51
Glacé icing 51
Rich chocolate icing 51

Royal icing 54—5
Whipped cream 51
Italian spaghetti 120

Jam cap pudding 37
Jamaican ginger loaf 63
Jelly fingers 93
Jelly oranges 93

Kebabs, cold 70
Kidney:
Amount to buy per person 14
Kidney soup 28
Liver and kidneys in red wine 104
Steak, kidney and mushroom pies 108
Steak and kidney pie 31
Steak and kidney pudding 32

Lamb:
To roast lamb 12
Lamb and apricot pudding 32
Lamb curry 106
Lamb with mustard sauce 112
Lardy cake 66
Leek:
Cream of leek soup 28
Lemon:
Blackcurrant and lemon refresher 116
Lemon curd cream 51
Lemon meringue pie 34
Lemon pudding 37
Lemon soufflé 27
Lemon suet pudding 38
Lettuce and celery salad 109
Liver. *See also* Pâté
Amount to buy per person 14
Liver and bacon parcels 121
Liver and gherkin triangles 72
Liver and kidneys in red wine 104
Lobster thermidor 102

Madeira cake 45
Malt loaf 62
Mandarin cloud 112
Mandarin gâteau 106
Mandarin jelly cake 96
Mayonnaise 25
Mayonnaise in blender 25
Mayonnaise, garlic 110
Meat. *See also* Beef, lamb etc.
To roast meat 12
To test if a joint is cooked 12
Amounts to buy per person 14
Gravy for roast meat 24
Meat balls with chutney sauce 70
Melon:
Compote of melon and black grapes 108
Melting moments 59
Meringues, plain and coffee 84
Milk shakes 116
Milk twist 64
Mince pies 34
Mocha whip 113
Mulled wine 114
Mulligatawny soup 28
Mushroom:
Cream of mushroom soup 28
Mushroom and chicken soup 117
Mushroom vol-au-vents 105
Onion and mushroom soufflé 25
Mustard sauce 24, 112

Noodles 104

Nuts and honey sandwiches 88

Oils for cooking 13
Onion:
Cream of onion soup 28
Onion and chicken liver flan 29
Onion and mushroom soufflé 25
Onion and pasta soup 117
Onion sauce 22
Open sandwiches 82
Orange:
Chicken and orange sandwiches 88
Jelly oranges 93
Mandarin cloud 112
Mandarin gâteau 106
Orange butter cream 50
Orange creams 97
Orange drizzle cake 95
Orange duck casserole 103
Orange glacé icing 51
Orange honey cream 51
Orange honey drink 114
Orange milk shake 116
Orange profiteroles 110
Orange pudding 37
Orange sandwich 45
Orange sauce 37
Orange soufflé 27
Orange sultana loaf 63

Paella 109
Pancakes:
Cherry almond pancakes 42
Dutch apple pancakes 41
Golden raisin pancakes 42
Honey banana pancakes 42
Pear and ginger pancakes 42
Parkin 48
Parsley sauce 22
Party mice 96
Pasta medley 120
Pasta supper dish 97
Pastry. *See also* Pies, tarts etc. *and*
turnovers
To bake pastry 'blind' 16
To prepare a flan case 16
Cheese pastry 16
Choux pastry 18
Flaky pastry 16
Flan pastry 16
Pastry edges 31
Pastry leaves 31
Rough puff pastry 18
Shortcrust pastry 16
Suet pastry 16
Pâté:
Chicken liver pâté 72
Chicken and pork pâté 73
Mixed fish pâté 73
Pea:
To cook peas 104
Pea and bacon soup 117
Peanut butter milk shake 116
Pear and ginger pancakes 42
Pear sundae 124
Peppermint butter cream 50
Pie:
Bacon and egg pie 29
Fruit pie 32
Lemon meringue pie 34
Mince pie 34
Steak, kidney and mushroom pies 108
Steak and kidney pie 31

Pilaff 121
Pineapple:
Bacon and pineapple flan 29
Ham and pineapple sandwiches 88
Iced pineapple cakes 42
Pineapple nut slice 77
Pineapple pudding 40
Pizza 66
Pizza special 119
Pizza tartlets 70
Plaice goujons with tartare sauce 70
Pork:
To roast pork 12
Chicken and pork pâté 73
Pork and apple pudding 32
Pork balls with chutney sauce 70
Pork paprika 111
Sweet and sour pork 105
Potato:
Baked jacket potatoes 111
Curried potato soup 119
Mashed potatoes 101
New potatoes 108
Potato scones 56
Super baked potatoes 97
Prawn mayonnaise tartlets 72
Prawns with garlic mayonnaise 110
Puddings:
Chocolate fudge pudding 41
Chocolate pudding 37
Christmas pudding 38
Fruit crumble 41
Ginger upsidedown pudding 39
Golden apricot crumble 96
Golden gooseberry crumble 124
Jam cap pudding 37
Lemon pudding 37
Lemon suet pudding 38
Orange pudding 37
Pineapple pudding 40
Sauces to serve with steamed puddings
37
Steamed fruit pudding 40
Steamed sponge pudding 37
Syrup pudding 37
Toffee sponge pudding 40
Puddings, savoury:
Beef and tomato pudding 32
Lamb and apricot pudding 32
Pork and apple pudding 32
Steak and kidney pudding 32

Queen cakes 42

Raspberry buns 44
Raspberry jam sauce 37
Ratatouille 101
Rice:
Boiled rice 106
Paella 109
Sausage and rice casserole 120
Savoury pilaff 121
Rock cakes 44
Rough puff pastry 18
Royal icing 54—5
Rum babas 67
Rum butter 38
Rum truffles 85

Salad:
Celery and lettuce salad 109
Crab and coleslaw salad 100
Fresh fruit salad 103

Fruit salad 73
Mixed green salad 103
Tossed green salad 112
Salad baskets 92
Waldorf salad 73
Salami and sweet pickle sandwiches 88
Salmon:
Cold salmon cutlets 72
Salmon crisp 121
Salmon and cucumber mousse 112
Salmon loaf 123
Smoked salmon rolls 70
Salted almonds 69
Sandwiches:
Continental sandwiches 88
Crispy sandwiches 92
Open sandwiches 82
Sandwiches for children's parties 88
Sangria 114
Sardine crumpets 121
Sauces:
Apricot jam sauce 37
Barbecue sauce 24
Béchamel sauce 24
Brown sauce 22
Caper sauce 24
Cheese sauce 22
Chocolate sauce 27
Curry sauce 24
Egg sauce 24
Garlic mayonnaise 110
Hollandaise sauce 24
Mayonnaise 25
Mustard sauce 24, 112
Onion sauce 22
Orange sauce 37
Parsley sauce 22
Quick tartare sauce 70
Quick tomato sauce 24
Raspberry jam sauce 37
Vanilla sauce 37
White sauce 22
Sausage:
Sausage cornets 92
Sausage pinwheels 90
Sausage and rice casserole 120
Sausage rolls 29
Savoury cheese tartlets 89
Savoury dips 88–9
Savoury pilaff 121
Savoury scones 56, 83
Scampi with tartare sauce 70
Scones:
Cheese scones 56
Cherry scones 95
Date and walnut scones 56
Dropped scones 58
Fruit scones 56
Girdle scones 56
Plain scones 56
Potato scones 56
Savoury scones 56, 83
Treacle scones 58
Welsh cakes 58
Sherry 113
Sherry trifle 74
Shortbread 58
Shortcrust pastry 16
Shrimp:
Cheese and shrimp dip 89
Shrimp and cheese flan 29
Tuna and shrimp cocktail 108
Simnel cake 46

Skye shortbread 58
Smoked fish turnover 31
Smoked salmon rolls 70
Soft drinks 113
Soufflés:
Savoury soufflés 25
Sweet soufflés 27
Soup:
Beef goulash soup 117
Chinese corn soup 117
Cream of carrot soup 28
Cream of cauliflower soup 28
Cream of celery soup 28
Cream of leek soup 28
Cream of mushroom soup 28
Cream of onion soup 28
Cream of vegetable soup 28
Creamed carrot soup 111
Cucumber soup 103
Curried potato soup 119
Frankfurt bean soup 117
Kidney soup 28
Mulligatawny soup 28
Mushroom and chicken soup 117
Onion and pasta soup 117
Pea and bacon soup 117
Special tomato soup 97
Tomato soup 27
Spaghetti:
Italian spaghetti 120
Sponge cake 48
Sponge drops 84
Sponge flan 39
Sponge pudding 37
Steak, kidney and mushroom pies 108
Steak and kidney pie 31
Steak and kidney pudding 32
Steamed sponge pudding 37
Strawberry:
Strawberry cream 116
Strawberry and grape rosettes 84
Strawberry palmiers 101
Strawberry treats 124
Stuffed eggs 83
Suet pastry 16
Sugar, types of 13
Summer punch 114
Sunshine snacks 120
Sweet and sour pork 105
Sweets:
Chocolate clusters 85
Chocolate fudge 97
Orange creams 97
Rum truffles 85
Truffles 97
Swiss meringue 124
Swiss roll 50
Syrup oat slices 35
Syrup pudding 37

Tartare sauce 70
Tarts, tartlets and flans:
Asparagus quiche 101
Cheese tartlets 28
Chicken and walnut tartlets 83
Crispy tartlets 89
Curried chicken tartlets 72
Dutch apple tart 34
Flan panachie 105
Frangipane flan 76
Pizza tartlets 70
Prawn mayonnaise tartlets 72
Rich Bakewell tart 32

Savoury cheese tartlets 89
Savoury flans 29
Sponge flan 39
Tea, to make 114
Teabreads:
Almond walnut loaf 96
Brack 63
Bun loaf 63
Cinnamon crunch loaf 63
Date and walnut loaf 62
Jamaican ginger loaf 63
Malt loaf 62
Orange sultana loaf 63
Toffee apples 94
Toffee bars 94
Toffee sponge pudding 40
Tomato:
Beef and tomato pudding 32
Quick tomato sauce 24
Special tomato soup 97
Tomato egg fluff 120
Tomato soup 27
Treacle scones 58
Trifle 74
Trifle-in-a-trifling 93
Truffles 85, 97
Tuna and shrimp cocktail 108
Turkey:
To roast turkey 12
Turnovers and pasties:
Bacon roll 29
Cream horns 35
Sausage rolls 29
Smoked fish turnover 31

Vanilla butter cream 50
Vanilla sauce 37
Vanilla soufflé 27
Veal:
To roast veal 12
Veal escalopes with ham and cheese 100
Vegetables. *See also* Asparagus, beans etc.
Amounts to buy per person 14
Cream of vegetable soups 28
Vermouth 113
Victoria sandwich 45
Viennese rosettes 44
Vol-au-vents 69, 105

Waldorf salad 73
Walnut:
Almond walnut loaf 96
Chicken and walnut tartlets 83
Coffee walnut cake 47
Date and walnut cake 46
Date and walnut loaf 62
Date and walnut scones 56
Honey and nut fluff 104
Walnut sandwich 45
Wedding cakes 78, 79
Wedding receptions 68
Welsh cakes 58
Whipped cream 51
White bread 64
White sauce 22
Wine 113
Wine cups 113
Wine, mulled 114

Yeast cookery 64–7
Yogurt jellies 95